AUTHOR STRAIGHT TALK

The possibilities, pit-falls, how-to's and tribal knowledge from someone who knows

SARAH GERDES

RPM Publishing

Library of Congress cataloging-in-publication data on file

Printed in the United States of America

978-1-54851175-3

First American Edition, 2017

P.O. Box 841 Coeur d'Alene, ID 83816

DEDICATION

For all aspiring or current authors who have questions no one will answer. You may not follow all the advice, wisdom or lessons-learned I share, but you will be informed in a way that I certainly wasn't when I started in publishing twenty years ago. May you skip the pain, collapse the years to market for your work and make more money than me.

CONTENTS

AUTHOR STRAIGHT TALK

INTRODUCTION

You don't have time to read, you want to write, I get it. I've been there. I know the anxious, I-can't-wait-to-get-started-and-get-my-book-out feeling. Along with this zeal come the questions that every aspiring author has: How do I get an agent or is an agent even required? What's the best route to market for my book? Where do I find a good editor? What if readers hate my book? When will I start making money?

This book came about because I have often wondered what would have happened if I'd had the advice, the insider information and tribal knowledge from agents, publishers, editors and other authors years ago, or even more recently. Would I have chosen a different publishing method? Hired editors earlier in the cycle? Used social media more effectively?

I hope my younger self would have read, listened and learned from all this insight, and I certainly hope you will too. **What you learn could save you years of frustration and money**.

Perhaps you are worried that this book will depress you with statistics, one more mental obstacle that stands between you and your future bestselling novel. I'll be clear: I do include real facts and figures that you need to know. The first one is that I was told by a publishing executive it's easier to become a professional athlete in the United States than a published author.

If this statistic bothers, you, I have one thing to say:

Read it, digest it, ignore it, and keep going, just as you did when you listened to your inner self who whispered that the idea in your head had merit and that you could do it. Jackie Collins wrote every one of her thirty-two bestselling novels on a yellow legal pad by hand. She was expelled in high-school yet sold over 500 million books in dozens of countries, proving that authoring is the great equalizer. One must not be a certain height, weight, color or even have a computer literacy level of a merit scholar to put an idea down on paper and turn it into a novel.

The only difference between the present you and that bestselling author you are looking up to is the commitment to write, and persistence to keep going when people tell you otherwise.

Today, most authors will tell you they spend forty-percent of their time actually writing. The other sixty percent of their day is spent on the business of authoring. I'll write that again. *Authoring is a business.* Any agent, publisher, movie producer or Broadway director is going to say the same thing. The sooner you get this into your head, the better off you will be down the road. The good news is that by reading this book, you have already mentally committed to pursuing your dream. Stop for a moment and reflect on that reality. You have taken action. You are making it happen. It may not always be easy or fun, but by placing one foot in front of the other, you are going towards your ultimate destination, not away from it.

Perhaps you won't agree with every point or principle, but know this: you are getting it straight from an author, hence the name. *Author Straight Talk* is the unfiltered truth from a person who has been through the cycles with mainstream and self-publishing, experienced multiple agents and editors, and had manuscripts optioned for movies and Broadway.

My only goal is to share my experience concisely so you know now what took me years to acquire. I'd also like you to:

- Avoid the mistakes and pitfalls common to authors
- Improve your chances of success in your genre
- Feel confident and assured as you pursue your dreams in the face of opposition

The Straight Talk Mindset

What you are writing is a product, not a book. It sounds harsh, but it's the truth, and every good agent, editor or producer refers to what comes out of your head and on to the written page as just that: a product to promote, sell and monetize. The sooner you start thinking of your finished manuscript as a product to sell to readers who can read it, the easier it will be to detach yourself emotionally so you can focus on the business of authoring.

The questions are posed exactly as I once asked, or as I've received them from others through Instagram, Facebook, unsolicited email and conversations. I've provided the answers, along with perspectives and alternative viewpoints from myself or others in the publishing, entertainment, or associated industry who have given me direct information. Most of the industry insiders who I quote (publishers, acquisition editors, agents) have asked for anonymity, as they are not authorized to go on the record for their organization. However, all supported my decision to share this information in order to help others. Why? By being better informed, you are actually helping them do their job.

What I won't give you

Tips on how to be a better writer, create storylines, improve your plot or deepen and strengthen your characters. Many other authors, agents and editors have produced amazing books and even YouTube videos on these aspects of writing. While I do share a few of my tried and proven favorite resources that have dramatically improved my writing, *Author Straight Talk* focuses on the business of authoring, where I pick out and share the most important feedback I've received, what helped and what didn't. At the request of aspiring authors, I include the emotional and philosophical aspects that have been necessary for me to endure the challenges unique to this profession.

It's my hope that you learn from my mistakes and perhaps will improve upon my successes. That would be awesome and I'd love to hear about it.

Book Organization

Chapter One: The Motivation, Money and Opportunity for your Book

1: Why write a book when so many are already out there?
2: How do I know if mine will be good enough?
3: What makes the best book?
4: Is it true the average self-published book makes less than $10,000 in its lifetime?
5: What's the tipping point then for sales?
6: My (self-published) book has sold less than fifty copies. I'm so demoralized, and even though I'm not doing it for the money, how do I handle this?
7: Do authors make money?
8: How long is the payout cycle?
9: You're telling me that even if I land on the New York Time's Bestseller list, it's still going to take two years for me to get paid?
10: What is considered a bestselling book?
11: What will agents take for commission?

Chapter Two: Inspiration, Insecurity and Writer's Block

12: I have a family and a crazy life. How can I possibly write?
13: I have physical disabilities. Can I still write a book?
14: I'm afraid my friends, family or members of my church will judge me. Is this normal?
15: I'm not confident enough to write a novel. Should I start with a short story and get it published before starting a novel?
16: I'm making money writing articles here and there. Can't I continue as I write my novel?
17: Where can I find inspiration?
18: Should I write about people, concepts and things I know?
19: How do I branch out from my own world without looking like a fraud?
20: What if nobody likes my novel?
21: I'm stuck, unable to write, and don't know how to start up again. Is Writer's Block real, and what can I do to get writing again?

Chapter Three: Bringing Your Book to Market

Chapter Four: Editing, the Difference Between Success and Failure

45: What should I expect to receive from an editor?
46: Is there more than one editing round?
47: How long does this editing round take and how much does it cost?
48: How are the bills typically paid?
49. So, in theory, I'm going to actually improve my writing by hiring an editor?
50: After the top-line, strategic editing, then what?
51: What's the difference between a line editor and a copy editor?
52: Will I have a different experience with an independent publisher, whom I'm paying to do all this work for me?
53: What can I realistically expect from an external editorial process?
54: How often should I expect to speak to my editor?
55: Do I wait until the entire manuscript is done or send in chapters?
56: If the proofreaders are so good, why do I still see errors in printed books I purchase?
57: I don't know anyone in the industry. Where do I start?
58: What's the total cost of getting my book to market, pre-marketing and sales?

Chapter Five: Process, Tools and Time Management

59: What is the best writing process to follow? It seems like every author, teacher, workshop and book I buy tells me to do something different.
60: What's after the outline?
61: What other processes exist to create a visual story flow?
62: Can't I just let it flow? I've read so much about writing this way and it's always talked about at conferences and writer's workshops.
63: What do I do with all the scenes that I've created (in my mind or on paper)?
64: How much does formatting play into the purchase of a book by a publisher?
65: Where does word count come into play?
66: Do I need a degree in creative writing?
67: Do I need a computer?
68: Should I take special classes to help improve my writing skills?
69: Do I backup my computer? What's a foolproof method?
70: Are there forums or events where I can connect with other authors in my genre?
71: What about attending a conference to meet a prospective agent or publisher?
72: I feel like my story is strong but my writing hasn't caught up. Any advice?

97: What are book ratings? Do I need them and do they have an impact on sales?
98: What about paying for reviews?
99: Does the number of reviews make a difference in book sales?
100: How do you get reviews?
101: Any tips on getting back of book quotes?
102: What role does a publicist play in marketing the book?
103: I wrote a novel and my agent is telling me it's not "in trend" anymore. Do I scrap it and write to the current trend?
104: What if I'm writing in a genre that doesn't exist—or at least not exactly. Is that impossible?
105: Do I need to keep writing in the same genre?
106: If I create my own genre, what are the challenges I'll face?
107: What are the benefits of a new genre?
108: If I have self-publish in a new genre (I've created) and the readers love the book, then why am I getting so much pushback from potential mainstream publishers?

Chapter Eight: Sales

109: I'm really naïve about pricing and conventions. What are the basics I should know about pricing?
110: What are good pricing strategies for a first-time author?
111: Should I write for the reader or myself?
112: How long before I become famous, and will this help my sales?
113: What about YouTube?
114: What will creating and managing a YouTube channel cost me?
115: When and how do book promotions come into play?
116: What are the details of a book give-away, and what are the best strategies for giveaways?
117: I don't have a ton of money to be purchasing books, then turning around and sending them to recipients. Any advice?
118: Can you show me how to run a giveaway promotion and what I should expect?
119: When and where do I use book discounts, and should discounts run concurrently with other promotions?
120: What's a true sign of a happy reader, and does this translate to sales?
121: What happens when sales get high enough to attract a tier three publisher, like an eBook only publisher? Should I consider it?
122: How do publishers assess the manuscripts provided by agents? In other words, does a ranking system exist?
123: Why are more and more authors creating their own imprint?

Chapter Nine: Author Career Options and Complimentary Revenue Streams

Chapter Ten: Ownership, Rights, Divorce and Estate

Questions for Sarah

151: How many books do you read on a monthly basis?
152: Do you watch movies, and how many per month?
153: Do you give out copies of your books as gifts?
154: Have you met any other famous authors?
155: How much time do you spend on research before you start writing?
156: Do you write all of your books in the same genres you read?
157: Will you stay a writer the rest of your life?
158: How do you handle a bad review?
159: What's the most stressful part of writing?
160: What's the most satisfying part of writing?
161: Should I subscribe to *Publishers Weekly?*
162: How much time do you spend writing versus marketing and sales?
163: Do you hire out your social media activities?
164: Do you have any author oddities that actually work?
165: What's the biggest downside of being an author?
166: Did you have an event that triggered your change in attitude?
167: Do you have any authors that you look to emulate (how they produce their content and control their brand)?
168: What skills do you recommend newbie authors develop ASAP?
169: Would you personally collaborate with any authors in the future?
170: How do you help other authors who you like, but don't want to collaborate with?
171: Any other genres you would seriously consider exploring and why?
172: Do you write on holiday?
173: If your book is getting made into a film, do you have any say? Why or why not?
174: Have you ever had an editor, publisher or director force you to include or changes your stories in ways that you have objected to?
175: Have you ever had any problems with crazy readers or people you've written about?
176: How do you deal with a person who strongly objects with something you've written in fiction or no fiction?
177: How do you keep your feet on the ground if you find success?
178: How do you keep the quality of your future writing and ideas high if you find success so that your brand is not ruined?
179: If writing is so hard to making a living from why do it in the first place?
180: Do you ever have moods where you can't write? What do you do about it?
181: How do you keep it fresh?
182: How much downtime do you have between writing books?
183: Do you have certain things you do during the downtime?
184: What advice do you give the most?

185: What's your biggest regret?

The Money, Motivation and Opportunity for Your Book

CHAPTER HIGHLIGHTS

- *Why write at all?*
- *Advances and royalties*
- *Commissions and payout schedules*

If you can't find a book you want to read, write it.

This immortal line, quoted by so many people including myself, I'm not sure can be attributed to any one person, nor should it be. The feeling is universal. Whether it's the dissatisfaction with current offerings or the lack of content in your area of interest, opportunity creates ideas, and ideas beget a product. The ultimate reason for writing, is of course, "I have a better idea." That's the start of this section, which focuses on the questions around the why of writing.

Question 1: Why write a book when so many are already out there?

Two answers. The first is Market Opportunity.

571 million books were sold in 2015[1]. Yes, million. That same year, forty-four thousand authors published over one million books, triple the number three years prior. Thus far, in 2017, I've written four books but during the same time, as a reader, I purchased over three dozen books, a mix of genres, fiction and trade (non-fiction) eBooks, hardbound and paperback. What does that tell you? The next book I buy could be yours.

The second answer is love and desire. You have a story inside you that's been on your mind for years. It aches to come out, it haunts you in your dreams. The books you read aren't nearly as interesting as your yet-unwritten story.

Former paramilitary soldier, divorced father and marketing specialist Andy Thomas wrote his first non-fiction book to help others quit smoking.

"I had struggled for so many years, I just wanted to help others." Self-published, it has sold 800 copies in short order, enough for him to gain the confidence to write his first novella. He's now writing his first full-length novel. "I never would have had the courage to write fiction if I hadn't been compelled by a need to help others first."

Question 2: How do I know if mine will be good enough?

---

[1] LA Times; book trends, December 31, 2015 on line issue

"You don't, but that's not the point," as my first fiction agent told me years ago. You write your book, complete it, send it off, get feedback from the industry or readers themselves, and you work hard to make the book even better.

The *point* is that you tried and succeeded in fulfilling your dream. Fear of failure or writing a mediocre book is what stops a potentially great author from starting in the first place. I delve into that quite a bit in later chapters, so for now, acknowledge its presence, give it a nod and put it in the corner. It's not going to go away for a while. **I'm on my thirteenth book and I still have plenty of fear.**

Question 3: What makes the best book?

"The best books written are those you want to read yourself," says my current fiction agent, Peter Rubie. To put this advice in context, Peter had already once fired me because he couldn't sell my fiction properties. He took me back after I approached him again having dramatically improved my writing. He basically asked: "What happened?" Followed by the exclamation: "You finally found your voice!"

I was mortified, because by this time I'd written seven books, four fiction and three non-fiction, but I told him the truth. I'd been through hell.

My daughter had gone through a serious health issue, during which time I'd broken multiple bones in my left leg which got infected and laid me up for six months. It required surgery and a pound of titanium to get my foot and leg working again, and I was just beginning to finally heal when my eldest brother committed suicide. After the funeral, my husband wanted to give the whole family a change of scenery, so we left town.

Sitting by the pool (because I couldn't actually be in the water yet), I craved a good book, but having been through the emotional, mental and physical wringer, the last thing I wanted to read was a book about angst, drama, infidelity and all sorts of negativity. I craved moral dilemmas where the heroine/hero chose the right path and ultimately found happiness because of their decisions.

"I wrote something I wanted to read," I finished telling Peter.

"That's what it took for you to find your voice. If you can't entertain yourself, you won't be able to entertain anybody else."

Does writing authentically mean one must experience drama, death, heartache in order to write about it? Nope, not at all. Think sci-fi and fantasy, where one author's imagination fills an entire book with wonderful characters and plots. Those writers wrote what they wanted to read, whatever the motivation, and did so successfully.

Peter ended with a congratulatory message. "You kept going until you found what worked." Had I given up earlier, I wouldn't have reached that point. "Don't give up, your best work is ahead of you," isn't just a trite phrase. It's the truth.

In life, finding a voice is speaking and living the truth. Each of you is an original. Each of you has a distinctive voice. When you find it, your story will be told. You will be heard.

John Grisham

Question 4: Is it true the average self-published book makes less than $10,000 in its lifetime?

Actually, the correct answer is **the average self-published book sells 257 copies and makes less than $1,200**. And therein lies the reason you, the author, are writing books for reasons other than fame and fortune.

Just two days ago an attorney told me he was writing a book.

"I'm not doing this for money," he was quick to say. "I'm doing it because I have a story inside me that's good enough to be told." This man was visiting with his seventeen-year-old daughter who is also an aspiring author.

"I love reading but I like writing more," said the attorney's daughter. "Plus, I think I write better than a lot of the stuff I read, so why shouldn't I give it a try?" She has completed over three hundred pages in her first novel and has five chapters to go.

This reflects the dominant reasons behind "the why?" question. An idea is inside you, begging to be told and you believe you can write it as well as, if not better, than anyone else.

Question 5: What's the tipping point for sales?

More on this in Chapter Five, but the short answer is a little tidbit that took me nearly two decades to learn. According to every agent, publisher and editor I've worked with, **the tipping point is eight books in any given category for sales to take off**. This is due to several factors:

- **Initial reluctance on the part of a reader.**

Apparently, most readers don't want to "get invested" in a new writer with only one, two or even three books. One editor likened it to going on a few amazing first dates, only to be ditched right after that, never having the second.

- **Readers want more, and they want them all now.**

Publishers have related to me that book sales in a series don't have the hockey stick effect until book three or four. E.g. books one and two sold modestly, but at book three, a reader will purchase 1-3 at once. The reader is assured the author isn't going to quit and not finish the series.

Historically, mainstream publishers will limit an author to one book a year. Readers, like myself, get understandably frustrated at waiting. When I come across an author I like, I will buy the whole multiple titles.

- **Once a reader finds an author they like, they consume the entire library.**

Off-hand remarks from various industry professionals have all given me examples of book sales skyrocketing between books seven and eight, regardless of the author or genre. From the publisher's perspective, "If an author makes it to eight books, we see sales of an entire library of titles in a single purchase."

On the other side, perhaps it's subconscious buying patterns that indicate a reader is likelier to invest in a new author with a lot of books. Regardless of why, the message is clear: write and create your library of books; eight is the golden number.

Question 6: My (self-published) book has sold less than fifty copies. I'm so demoralized, and even though I'm not doing it for the money, how do I handle this?

> Statistics don't take into account a person's desire, commitment, aptitude and hard work. In authoring, success isn't due to a roll of the dice. 85% is due to hard work and putting in long hours.

Let's face it, at our core, humans want and need to be validated, especially creative people. When a consumer pays hard-earned money for a product, it's validation that the product is worthwhile, even if only a dozen copies are sold. Take heart that a few copies were purchased, instead of none at all.

We will get to the reasons why your book isn't selling in later chapters, be it the (bad) writing, little or no editing, or zero marketing—or a combination of the three. In the meantime, you need to do one thing:

Tell yourself there is a reason you are here: **you are being asked, prompted, encouraged and inspired to do something that is hard and requires a lot of diligence and persistence.** Don't give up. Keep going. That's what I told myself for years, and it's paid off.

Question 7: Do authors make money?

Yes, but it varies on the price, the royalty agreement, the format and length of the book and the sales territory (country).

I'm going to break it down and describe the three primary variables that determine whether an author makes money. I'll do so by using one of my first books as the example because the data is real and current.

- **Publishing entity sets the cover price & royalty scale**

The price is based upon a variety of factors, the most important being the length and format of the book. For *Navigating the Partnership Maze: Creating Alliance That Work*, a non-fiction Trade (or business) title, the hardbound price was $27.99. McGraw-Hill set the price and informed me it would discount the retail price based upon various channels (such as the education market, which receives a flat 60% off the retail price). My royalty per book wouldn't change with the channel.

Table 1. Hardcover royalty model

Book	Format	Distribution	Royalty
Navigating the Maze	Hardcover w/flap	Traditional (bookstores)	$1.75/book
Navigating the Maze	Paperback	China only	.08 cents/book
Navigating the Maze	Paperback & eBook	Not offered	Not offered

Romance, suspense and action adventure are fiction, but non-fiction authors such as those writing and cookbooks I know have all been given similar contracts with one caveat: **the page count**

flexibility increases in direct correlation to the success of the author in certain fiction genres. Read that again, please. Certain genres only. This doesn't typically apply to non-fiction (also called Trade), where reader buying patterns and book format is tried and proven.

- **Page count**

Many publishers will set the page count. It varies with the genre. For my non-fiction book, I was given a "not to exceed" page count. In fact, the contract stipulated that a manuscript submitted with a page count over this number would be rejected.

- **Advances**

Publishers have guidelines for advances which have dramatically dropped in the last decade. Unless you are a personality or well-known figure with an established following, the advances are low or non-existent.

For example, for *Navigating the Maze* (2001), my advance was $15,000. That was considered high at the time for a first-time author in the non-fiction trade category. As Matt Wagner, my agent then at Waterside Communications told me, the deal was made so quickly because I met all four of the criteria established by McGraw-Hill internal.

This was later confirmed by the acquisitions editor during our discussion.

1. I had a reputation as an expert in my field (quoted in magazines, television expert, etc.).
2. My speaking schedule was robust: I was speaking at about

dozen or more events around the country/overseas per year.

3. My network of contacts and database was large, and the publisher assumed mentions in my newsletter, articles and other materials would drive sales.
4. Those I interviewed in the book would purchase some certain % of copies, and their own extended network would do the same.

In other words, the publisher (and the marketing team therein) ran the numbers and figured that even with the advance, it would then take a certain number of sales of the book to recoup the money. Given my background, they were confident they could reach that number of sales, thereby earning back the money they paid me and more. This is one reason why non-fiction books are easier to get published for a first-time author.

The schedule for the advance for *Navigating the Partnership Maze* looked like this:

Table 2. Advance payout schedule

Format	Advance	Payout 1	Payout 2	Payout 3
Hardcover	$15,000	$5,000 "upon signing". Arrived 45 days after the contract was signed.	$5,000 upon formal acceptance of the submitted manuscript.	$5,000 upon publication
		Check arrived in 90 days		When the book hit the stores

While I'm on the section of advances, I'm going to share with you the advance payments for my action adventure series, *Chambers*. While the first book didn't find a mainstream US Publisher (reasons later revealed), it was picked up by three foreign publishers in

Indonesia, Poland and Thailand within four weeks of the Frankfurt Book Fair. Two advances were $2,500 while the third was $1,250. These were paid in full, within sixty days of the signed contract. The royalty per book averages $2.75 across the three territories. Territories is the commonly used phrase in publishing, film and media so it's what I'll use referring to foreign countries.

- **Bonuses and Accelerators**

Outside the niche of business development and increasing sales, I wasn't well known by the public. McGraw-Hill included a bonus structure for an increase in the royalty for reaching certain sales milestones. My contract stipulated that for every 5,000 books sold, I received a bump in the royalty paid. When sales hit 15,000, the contract stipulated a unit royalty of $3.00/book, almost doubling my royalty rate prior to that sales level.

Question 8: How long is the payout cycle?

Let's start from the time of submission. Books typically have an 12-18-month editorial, printing, marketing and distribution cycle. Your book is slotted into a timeline for each phase, and the resources required are assigned. Without unforeseen calamities (natural disasters, terrorist attacks) or the basic personnel changes that can occur within a publishing house, your book will hit the market 24 month after your final manuscript draft has been accepted.

Now let's look at the entire publishing process, from submission to monetary payout.

Table 3. Mainstream publishing timeline

Milestone	Date	Notes
Submit your manuscript	Publisher accepts	Editing, marketing, printing, distribution
18 month sales cycle (12 months)	January 15, 2018	Publishers allow retail stores up to 12 months before reporting is required
Retail reports to the publisher	June 15, 2018	If the retail store chooses to report earlier they can do so
Hold-back (reserve) period	January 15, 2019	Publishers hold-back money received for a period, 6-12 months, to allow for returns. Readers can return a book regardless of the length of time (usually) up to 12 months for a refund or exchange. Publishers will do one of two things: one, pay the author and then account for returns by taking money out of future royalty payments or two, hold-back the royalty for being paid for up to twelve months.
Final reporting Year One	June 15, 2019	Once the publisher closes out the year, the check is made to the agent of record.
Agent takes commission, cuts check to the author	July-Sept 15, 2019	The agent can take 30-90 days to cut the check to authors. My experience has been just this; the agent process varies, but it's never more than 90, except when foreign.
Total time to get paid from date of publication	2.5 years, or 30 months	

This is one the main reasons that mainstream authors—those who have publishers with names like Harper-Collins, Simon and Schuster and others--have created imprints and are self-publishing. **The cycle is approximately 3-4 years from the time you submit the book to when you receive your first check.**

I'm excluding the deals and payout schedules for celebrities and former politicians (think Obama, Clinton etc.) who get pushed ahead of scheduled authors for both editing, printing, distribution and payouts.

Now comes the waiting. Publishers haven't caught up with the digital times, nor have retailers changed their archaic rules about returns, royalties and payments. Since this very book you are reading is under my own imprint, I can boldly proclaim an opinion that is shared by thousands of authors and agents around the world: the timeframes, processes and protocols of mainstream publishing are ridiculous and antiquated.

> **Hold-Back**: In publishing, it's also referred to as 'reserves.' This means that even though your books have sold and you are due a royalty check, the publisher is making the decision to *hold-back* that money in case of future returns.

Question 9: You're telling me that even if I land on the New York Time's Bestseller list, it's still going to take two years for me to get paid?

That's right, unless you're in that rarified group with a unique contract, which is unlikely because you're reading this book. Now you know why so many authors published by mainstream houses (Simon & Schuster, Harper Collins, Scholastic, et all) have moved to self-publishing. This alternative avenue allows authors to get paid almost immediately once a threshold of $100.00 per day is hit.

A great example of this is Brandilyn Collins, who had over 30 romance and suspense books published by Harper-Collins. Five years ago (approximately 2012) she started requesting the copyrights back from earlier titles and simultaneously began her own imprint. She published nearly a dozen books under her own publishing company and couldn't be happier.

"I have the control, the process down and the ability to get more royalties much faster than I had under my publisher."

Question 10: What is considered a bestselling book?

For hard-cover, non-fiction trade, 15,000 copies sold is considered great. I've had publishers tell me at that point, a second edition may be ordered and the book will be touted at foreign books fairs. If sales are constant, a two-book deal is likely to be offered. Within fiction, it seems to depend on the genre. Generally, publishers, editors and agents have repeated that when a fiction book sells over 30,000 copies it's considered a major hit, particularly if it's in the young adult, middle grade or picture book categories. When a book reaches 60,000 copies, regardless of the genre, publishers are begging for sequels and more books from that author.

It only takes 5,000 book sales to make it to the New York Times Bestseller list.

Question 11: What will agents take for commission?

Most agency-author agreements stipulate between fifteen to twenty percent commission and zero money up front. For this, the agent will sometimes (not always, I've learned) read your book, provide feedback, create the list of publisher targets in tiers, starting with the top three. I've had agents go all the way down to what has been identified as tiers four and five, then eBook publishing houses only. More on that in Chapter three.

To date, I've signed four agency agreements, one agent per company, specializing in my areas. The contracts ranged between fifteen and twenty percent, all for agents located in the United States. Foreign agent agreements start at twenty percent, and this is on-top of the US agent commissions.

Cutting checks to the author is about operational costs and efficiency, not the size of your check or the immediacy of getting it to you. Be patient. The hold-up is likely at the publisher side, not the agent.

Not always, I will state, but *generally*. What that means is that I worked with my domestic and foreign agent(s) and they cut the fees from 40% down to a more reasonable 25-30%. In other words, when a book of mine is sold in a foreign territory, thirty percent is getting cut right off the top, split between both agents.

Agents use a variety of schedules to cut commission checks: quarterly, bi-annually or annually. When the money is large and the publisher sets the timelines, the agents adjust accordingly.

In Issaquah, Washington, I met a librarian for the city who is also a romance author. She falls in the category of the paperback market listed above. Her publisher prints a single run of 100,000 copies and she earns between .20 and .80 cents per book, no accelerators or bonuses, and no second editions. To date, she's written seven books, all published under a pen name. They are "Bodice-ripping, ecstasy-driven period books," she practically squealed with delight. This woman stands just over five feet tall and is nearly as wide. Still, her vibrant personality shines as bright as her honesty.

"I don't do it for the money," she explained, her smile wide. "I do it for the men!" Of course, being the curious soul that I am, I had to ask further.

> **An author's rule**: the best books are the ones you want to read yourself.

"Here, I'm nobody. I'm not married and never get asked out on a date, but when I attend a romance author's event, we all get dressed up in our period clothes and all these half-naked male models surround me and put their arms around me. It's wonderful!" She also added that because she uses a pen name, no one in the local area has a clue as to her alter identity as an author, which gives her true freedom of expression in her writing, but also at these author events she attends.

"I get treated like a rock star, if you want to know the truth." The adoring fans know her under her pen name (which she asked I not reveal so I can share her experience honestly), and are completely uninhibited when speaking with her. "They will tell me which sex scenes they like the best and why, and pretty soon, I know all the most personal details of their lives."

She bonds with her readers on a level most of us will never experience, and it satisfies her otherwise mundane life. She writes between two and three titles a year, the page count is roughly 225 per book. Yes, she has a formula for her books as it relates to the heroine, the hunk, the bad guy or girls, and the ending. She is completely unapologetic.

"My reader knows what he or she is going to get when they buy my book, and I never get tired of telling the storylines."

Still, I couldn't help but go back to the subject of money. Did she earn enough to make a living or increase her savings account?

"Some books will sell eighty thousand copies, other books only ten, but since I have my day job, it's a fun second income which is the way I look at it."

She also doesn't care about awards or fame, which is helpful as she writes under a pen name. She has her priorities and her focus and is content with her lucrative second career, as she calls it.

"I won't ever be the famous person on the street and I'm great with that. I don't want the pressure of people knowing me, judging me and pressuring me about what I choose to write. I'm writing this for me, doing it for me and am lucky enough to get paid some money and treated well. What more could I ask for?"

Not much.

Extra data on popular genres

Table 4. Advance and royalties by genre

Genre	Advance	Royalties	Notes
Romance (paperback)	$2,500-$4,500 offered	$.80 cents per book	A single print run of 100,000 copies. No accelerators or bonuses.
Romance (hardcover)	$1,500.00 (first-timers) $5,000 for published authors	$1.25/book	Advance and royalties based upon the genre and author.
Cookbooks (hardcover)	$2,500-10,000	$1.20-$2.30/book	Accelerators are common and based upon sales
Children's picture books (hardcover)	$1,250-$5,000	$.80-$2.50/book	The majority of this goes to the illustrator
eBooks- all categories	$1,250-$5,000	$.50-$4.00	eBook only publishers

Inspiration, Insecurity & Writer's Block

CHAPTER HIGHLIGHTS

- *Making time*
- *Overcoming & succeeding*
- *Permissions & infringement*

If I waited for perfection, I'd never write a word.

Margaret Atwood

Making time to write is a constant struggle for most of us. A perfect schedule lasts for a point in time. Life intrudes, with family, career changes, moving, marriage, you name it. My daily schedule has changed more times than I can count and continues to do so, with fall (think school), vacations and summer (I want to play, not write), and even the holidays, where cooking and entertaining take over my life.

So how do I do it? And by "it" I mean, continue to write and release books on a regular schedule with a family of four, a dog, cat, 23 chickens and a duck.

Easy. I make setting aside writing time a priority, and I'm going to show you how to do the same. Then I'm going to reveal the insecurity and fear that comes along with this craft, emotions that affect every person I know who is what I call a "creative." **We create, therefore we feel, and because we feel, we fear rejection, judgement from others and all sorts of things peculiar to our vocation**. Lastly, when one is creative, the lives, stories, music and details of other people's lives are used for inspiration. We must be authentic while using discretion.

Question 12: I have a family and a crazy life. How can I possibly write?

You start with twenty minutes a day. That's it.

Years ago, I read that Stephen King wrote for eleven hours a day. Wow, I thought, he's a machine. Pre-marriage, pre-kids, pre-distractions, I, too, could devote hours at a time to writing. As the years progressed, the hours reduced to single digits, then half-hour blocks, then stopped entirely. **It wasn't because I didn't actually have time to write, it was because I had set my personal expectation so high it was unattainable**. If I couldn't spend four hours and "get into my story," I wasn't going to bother. It was like exercising. If I couldn't go to a 90-minute class, then I'd not exercise at all.

With age, came wisdom. I evaluated my daily allocation of time and was appalled at all the unused (e.g. poorly used) hours I frittered away. I cooked, cleaned, socialized with my husband, skied in the winters and played tennis in the summers. When I conducted an honest assessment of my day, I realized I had more than enough hours to carve out twenty minutes a day for my writing.

Let me write that again. *Twenty. Minutes. A. Day.*

In twenty minutes, an author can write about five paragraphs of first draft quality.

Excuses. Excuses. "I can't get into the story if I don't have at least an hour," was one phrase I'd use. Another favorite was: "I'll never get to my goal if I don't write a page a day," then I'd give up entirely.

It wasn't until I fully committed to twenty-minutes a day did I realize my excuses were just that—excuses—geared to cover up my fear of failure. With that in mind, I took my computer with me and wrote on the plane, in the foyer waiting for my doctor's appointment. Anywhere I could work for twenty minutes. If I wrote daily (and that was the key) I could immediately start up where I'd left off the day before.

Think of it this way. In twenty minutes, you can accomplish the following:

- Walk a mile on a treadmill
- Make a cake
- Take a shower and do your hair
- Watch a television show

- Read two chapters in a book

You could also be writing a page a day, which translates to 365 pages of a first draft over the course of a year. Chapter Five delves into extended schedule management and provides examples of other author's time allocation. But for now, keep it simple. Twenty minutes.

Question 13: I have physical disabilities. Can I still write a book?

Unequivocally, the answer is yes. Let me share one woman's journey.

Her name is Rachel Parker, and one day she appeared on my Instagram account. Periodically, I search authors and quotes, and when I found her account, I liked several of her posts and commented. She responded, rather excited, because she couldn't believe it was me (she'd read *Chambers*, one of my books) and was so thrilled she'd been recognized and validated. Over the next few months, I learned more about her story. She's twenty-eight and suffers from periodic vision loss due to migraines. She has debilitating arthritis and diabetes, and a host of other things that tore my heart apart. She is in physical pain when she looks at the bright screen of the computer and her fingers burn when she types.

Yet, type she does, as often as her body allows. I encouraged her to try twenty-minute blocks, and this works on the good days. Over the last year, she has worked hard on her first full-length novel and is near completion.

If she can do it, you can do it. No more excuses. Twenty minutes.

Question 14: I'm afraid my friends, family or members of my church will judge me. Is this normal?

Not only is this normal, it should be expected. Just wait, because people really get weird when your first book is picked up by a mainstream publisher. It changes again once reviewers start writing about how great your book is because you suddenly become "legitimate," no longer an aspiring author but a "real author," which, in itself, is a put-down.

John Grisham was quoted as saying the members of his church were his worst critics. He wisely didn't get into the reasons for their criticism, but they probably echo what I've heard from fellow authors and experienced myself. People feel jealousy, envy and insecurity around regular, non-authors. A few other specific issues will come up that you should be prepared to encounter.

- Every person will think you are writing about them.

It's funny and sad and true, and likely contributes to writers becoming more introverted as time goes on. The fact is that people, experiences and situations are potential fodder for your creativity. You can address this upfront by joking that you "don't write about people you know," or you "don't write about people in a twenty-mile radius." I've used all sorts of quips to allay this initial fear and concern.

- Fame does funny things to others and you can't control it.

For some reason, when I was "just a businessperson," no one cared about the book I'd written for McGraw-Hill, or that I'd spoken at Harvard and had been on all the major news stations giving my expert advice. I suspect this was because it was antiseptic business commentary and wasn't cool. At the end of the day, I had to get up, brush my teeth and go to work just like everyone else.

Come up with a few quips that can be used when a person learns you are an author, either aspiring or published. It will help diffuse their initial judgement and assure the individual you can keep your relationship with them separate from your works.

This changed when I began writing full time and my fiction work started taking off. I was told I was more stand-offish, and I probably was, but it had nothing to do with ego. I got tired of being introduced to a new person, that individual asking about my life, my saying I was an author (revealing nothing about my business background) and then seeing a mental and sometimes physical distance go up between us. A certain wariness would fill the person's eyes, and that was it.

At church, fellow congregants refused to read my books and I was told it was because "Sarah has enough stars in her life, she doesn't need more." At my children's school, I kept my mouth shut and was generally known for being a stay-at-home mom. Thankfully, I recently moved to a very small town where the big news of the day is the number of moose crossing the local river. No one cares about me being a published author.

While the reasons for *why* a person will react to you being a writer will change with your success, the feelings associated with how people respond to you won't. Accept that these negative aspects are associated with your vocation of choice and continue to write.

Keep your head down, fingers on the computer and write. Ignore the naysayers, the skeptics, the friends, church patrons or family members who provide nothing but negativity. Your story is the only one that counts. Write it.

Question 15: I'm not confident enough to write a novel. Should I start with a short story and get it published before starting a novel?

Absolutely, positively not. If you want to write novels, start writing novels. Everything else is a distraction until you perfect your craft. That's not to say that articles and even blogs have a place, time and reason for being and I'll share more about that in Chapter 7 on Process Improvement.

John Le Carre is often pointed to as an example of a wonderfully successful author who began his career writing short stories. But what no one brings up is that he spent years perfecting short story writing; years he could have spent writing the novels for which he later received so much acclaim (and he was quoted as admitting he was fearful of failing at being a novelist, so he took up short stories).

To make this personal, I spent hours/months of my life blogging, which I enjoyed because it "kept my mind sharp." That's what I told myself. My voice of honesty, otherwise known as my husband, called me out.

"You're hiding," he said bluntly, then left the room. He was right. **I was hiding behind the blog, running away from writing a novel**. Blogs are fun, easy and time consuming, and they have zero impact on writing my books and *perfecting my craft.*

That's a phrase that I've heard time and time again from my agents and editors. My ideas were always great, it was my inability to write well that proved to be my stumbling block. It persisted because I got caught in the trap that I'd "start small" and write my way up to novels.

Don't fall into that trap. Be clear about what you are writing and focus on that pursuit.

Question 16: I'm making money writing articles here and there. Can't I continue as I write my novel?

I'm also going to include "making money writing short stories" in the above question.

You can do anything you want, but it will come at a cost. Let me share an experience, because I fell into this trap as well.

In my twenties, a published article in a regional or national magazine paid well, about $1,200 per article (which is a far cry from what's paid today). Writing articles also came easy to me. I'll skip over the details, but suffice it to say within months of cold-calling the editor of a regional magazine, I'd been published in *Alaska Airlines Magazine*, *Salt Lake City Magazine*, *Catalyst Magazine*, *Healthcare Informatics* and quite a few others. At the time, I told myself I'd do both; work on my novel and write the articles, dividing my time in equal parts.

Life never works out quite the way you hope. Furthermore, I thought that I could add to my writing resume by giving short stories a shot. An editor of a national magazine gave me a chance and asked me to write a short story on spec. That means I'd write the piece and if he liked and published it, I'd get paid. If not, no deal. After I sent it in, he kindly informed me that if my goal were to be an author of novels, and not short story fiction, I was wasting my time.

"Starting today, it will take you years to perfect this craft and there isn't much money in it," he said. "So, unless you are intending on eventually compiling all your short stories into a single book, which by the way you can't do if we purchase the story and own the copyright, then you should focus elsewhere."

Oh, I thought to myself. That wasn't really what I had in mind. I graciously thanked him for saving me years of wasted effort and have never attempted to write another short story since.

If you want to be an author of novels, write novels and forget about the short story format.

Question 17: Where can I find inspiration?

Everywhere. When I see an interesting face, observe an unusual situation, participate in a unique event, hold a spirited conversation, have a memorable dream—it's all fodder for my novels.

Speaking of dreams, Stephenie Meyer said her inspiration for Twilight came to her in a dream. I believe it's because our subconscious is free from the confines of our rational day-light self that precludes creative thinking. If your life is filled with friends, work and noise of all types, it's hard to be really and truly quiet so you can be open to your inner self. Remember, nothing that happens to a writer is ever wasted, it's all reused, massaged and tailored for a story.

Beyond dreams, I do have a few top inspirational venues that continue to be ripe for creativity.

> Create a writing folder with your ideas for books and keep adding your notes until you write the book. The descriptions and details will be authentic and accurate.

- **Conversations**

People are the most interesting sources of ideas and conversations are revealing. For an upcoming book on success, I interviewed a man who had built a $700M business. I asked him to describe his key(s) to success. "Having a conversation," he replied, without hesitation. He said he could learn everything he needed—be it how to decide a deal, hire a person, or create a product, just by having a conversation. "I ask a question then shut up and listen until they talk themselves out." I've found it works that way in authoring as well.

- **Locale**

Author Andy Thomas lives in Northern Britain, not far from the seaside cliffs that served as the inspiration for Bram Stoker's Dracula. Andy said his first novella in the paranormal genre was inspired by the surrounding areas because it's spooky, mysterious, and happens to be where he takes his daily runs.

- **Hardship**

For some reason, God granted me a whole lot of personal failures to compensate for the success I've had in my professional life. Most, if not all, of what I write is grounded in the seeds of hardship. To go one step further, I'm honest enough to admit that when I'm mentally down and emotionally strung out, I'm more open minded. It's strange but true. It's then that I become quiet and just listen to everything around me.

- **Travel**

Foreign or domestic, exotic or simple, I put the phone away (entirely, 100%) and take only a little notebook and my favorite pen. Once I'm relaxed, the ideas start pouring forth. I now commonly outline, chapter by chapter, an entire book on vacation. To me, **it's not work, it's creative freedom**. Honestly, it's my favorite part of the whole process. Sometimes, it's my favorite part of the entire vacation.

- **Tip: Keep a writing folder**

I started collecting articles and pictures on St. Moritz, Switzerland three years before I came up with the story line for *A Convenient Date*, which has a few chapters set in Switzerland. I kept adding to the folder, and then finally, about five years after I'd started my research, I spent a month in Europe, two weeks of it in Switzerland. I wrote *Date*, and the following year, I traveled again to Europe and this begat the basis for a three-book series. Two were published last year.

Five years is a long time, you might be saying to yourself, but that's nothing to *Chambers*, an action adventure series I'm writing. While in college, I took a history class and became enamored with a civilization in South America believed to have been the first giants recorded at about 8 feet tall. The ruins, culture and traditions of these people became the essence for the story line of *Chambers*, but much of that isn't revealed until the last few books of the series. The legend, however, served as the basis for the storyline.

Question 18: Should I write about people, concepts and things I know?

No, not necessarily, and I'll say upfront that I have a philosophical difference with probably half of the industry professionals that I know regarding this topic. While I concur that sometimes a scene or character comes across as more genuine if the author has a tangible, first-person experience with a person, place or thing, I don't believe it's a requirement. On one hand, you have Ann Rice, who set her vampire series in New Orleans, where she lived and could bring the crypts to life along with the neighborhoods. On the other hand, you have Stephenie Meyer, who said she never stepped foot in Forks, Washington, yet set her Twilight series there and it's as real as any other place I've read about.

While I've been to all the locations in my women's general interest books, it was impossible to do so for my action adventure series and non-fiction autobiography. How could I? That would mean time traveling back to China in the 1500's and the 1940's in South Korea. Instead, I spent a month conducting research and allowing my imagination to fill in the blanks of the missing details. I won't lie. It was hard, but both projects came together in the end in a way that pleased me.

> **For your first project**, it would be ideal if you write a manuscript in a genre that fits your writing style and knowledge base and any research that needs to be conducted can be done at your local library or on the Internet.

If you are unsure, then yes, start by writing what you know, if it's pleasing to you, because you are the most important reader. On the other hand, if your world is uninteresting, then fantasize about the world you *want* to live in, the one that makes you bound out of bed in the morning and stay up far too late at night. If that other place is exciting to you, it will likely to appeal to others.

Question 19: How do I branch out from my own world without looking like a fraud?

You give it a shot, complete the book and either submit it to your agent or continue with another publishing method. If the manuscript is rejected by your agent for being unauthentic, then you know you must work a bit harder. I've experienced this myself.

When I decided to add fiction to my non-fiction library, I had this ideal of being the female version of Robert Ludlum, one of my favorite authors. I loved his fast-paced, strong characters with an element of suspense, action and romance. My non-fiction agent didn't represent fiction and so introduced me to Peter, a Brit who came to New York after working on Fleet Street, had several well received books to his name and a long list of top selling authors under his representation. He finally accepted me as an author after 15,000 copies of my first self-published book sold to schools and local bookstores in the State of Washington. After several of my manuscripts in the same genre were rejected, he was blunt.

"Sarah," Peter said. "What are you trying to write?" Ludlum, I recall telling him, summarizing all that I had dreamed about for decades. "But you're not good at it." When I told him I didn't want to write anything else, he pulled out the big guns.

"Well, I can't sell what you're giving me, so go back and try again in another genre." Ouch!

I had no choice. And so I sat down to write what I considered bubble gum fiction and submitted it to Peter. While he was thrilled I'd "found my voice," a part of me was genuinely depressed. Understanding my dilemma, he sought to give me another perspective.

"Look at it this way," he began, "You like to cook, right? You have this vision of being a Michelin-starred chef, making Coq au Vin, but you aren't any good at it. What you are really good at is making pizza." He continued, ignoring my gasp of mortification. "It's downscale to you. Maybe even embarrassing, but guess what? More people eat pizza than a dish they can't pronounce. Write what you are good at. Embrace it."

Readers, that advice was not easily taken to heart. It has taken me the last four years to come to terms with the fact that I'm never going to be the author I wanted to emulate, but I couldn't deny his words had truth. **The publishers didn't want what I was creating and I had a choice: stop writing, adapt, or write for an audience of one. Me**.

The epilogue? Peter was right, again. I learned to adapt and my women's fiction has outsold all my other books.

Question 20: What if nobody likes my novel?

Is "nobody" your mother, who, like mine, reads my women's fiction with the obligation of a parent? She really doesn't care for my books and only muscles through my work out of obligation, but she is at least honest and tells me so.

Since you have probably guessed that my first piece of advice on this topic is going to be a variation of keep writing and ignore the external voices around you, my second suggestion is to develop a thick skin. Family members are the harshest critics following by agents. Publishers have a modicum of professionalism, because they know at some point you may write a manuscript they want. Scorched Earth doesn't usually recover.

Develop a Thick Skin: Agents and publishers can be harsh, but family members are often the worst—not because of what they say, but because their opinion matters and you are emotionally involved with them. Sometimes it's better to say nothing at all to relatives and let the sales of your book do the talking.

Let me go back to the harshest critics and naysayers of an aspiring author: family members. Just this week, I had a conversation with a woman who recounted how her father dismissed her first book, one she'd written in high school, and then did so again this past year, when the woman self-published her first adult novel. The author said it was like ripping open an old wound.

The woman is 42, a math teacher who wrote a fantasy novel that has the most interesting plot line I've seen in a long time. In addition to her father, her younger sister chimed in on Facebook and essentially knocked her for trying to write a book this late in life. I guess no one told her that James Patterson started writing novels when he was in his fifties.

This gets back to the point of "nobody likes it." Negativity is going to come from all sides. **To prevent depression, take an**

objective view of the source of the criticism. Was it an editor in your genre who has a track record of bestsellers, or the wife of your son's football coach? When I reframed my mother's comments, I discovered it wasn't my writing she didn't like, nor the storylines, because she thought both were good. Her dislike centered on the characters themselves.

"I want more drama, more angst," she has told me time and again. "People's lives don't always turn out right, and they should have more flaws." For the record, my characters have plenty of flaws, but obviously not enough for my mother, a former shrink who has seen and counseled the worst of society.

"Mom," I respond patiently, "people, including myself, have enough drama and downers in their life. I don't need to write more of it."

Once I got to the heart of my mother's comments, I felt remarkably better. At my core, I'm an optimist and maintain that most things can be achieved through perseverance and hard work. This comes through in my novels, no matter the genre: business, action-adventure or women's fiction. While I craved my mother's approval, I recognized that I don't, and won't likely ever, write books that will appeal to her. And now I'm at peace with that because a whole bunch of other people read and like my works.

Question 21: I'm stuck, unable to write, and don't know how to start up again. Is Writer's Block real, and what can I do to get writing again?

When I was twenty-six years old, I was given a book by Melody Haller, a veritable legend in the San Francisco world of public relations. It was invaluable to me during my first few years of writing. It's called *100 Days of Creative Writing*. This has lifted me out of the trenches of writer's block, which is a fancy phrase to describe a lack of direction or a stall in ideas.

When you have gone through all 100 ideas, the best cure for the creative stall is to keep writing. It's akin to the airplane that's going up, stalls and starts to go down. The pilot adjusts, maneuvers and gets the plane out of the stall, all the while still flying. We push through the empty spots in our lot, even if the "spark" of brilliance is lacking. Write the scene anyway and come back to it later, improving each time through the revision process. Doing so prevents the tendency to stop writing altogether. **An afternoon of inactivity leads to a day, then a week, and soon you've gone a month without writing a word, and it's blamed on writer's block**.

Don't fall into that trap. One aspiring writer, a mother of three, was half-way through a brilliant novel and called me in desperation.

"What do I do?" she wailed, confessing it had been days since she'd even attempted to write.

"Get back on it and keep going," I answered, without a hint of sympathy. The brain works all the time, not just when you are at the computer. You must actively keep your mind focused on the project/scene/resolution for the creative brain to manifest a solution to a problem you're facing. Don't let writer's block, or the creative stall, prevent you from getting closer to your goal of a completed manuscript. Get up, get dressed and get writing. The solution will come.

Question 22: Can I change genres if I get writer's block?

Of course, you can do whatever you want as an author, but before you give up, consider going through an exercise first. This was recommended to me by Jennifer Fisher, a former acquisitions editor at a big, mainstream publishing house in New York.

The Author Promise: Determine what you are going to give the reader, deliver it and never break that promise.

I'd hit my own wall of writing, and hit it hard. Peter suggested I reach out to an editor and recommended Jennifer. She said one thing to me which has been my guiding light ever since.

"Determine what you want to give reader, your unspoken promise, and never break it. If you do, they will flee and never come back."

Not only was this a necessary exercise in thinking about what I was going to write—and how readers would perceive me—but it was core to "building the brand" of the author, Sarah Gerdes, fiction and non-fiction alike.

The second benefit of Jennifer's suggestion was that I was reinvigorated with energy, focus and passion. Suddenly I was crystal clear on my authoring mission.

Ray Bradbury famously said: "You only fail if you stop writing." Keep going, push through and never stop. Your dream becomes reality when you take action to keep going while others give up.

Question 23: Should I use a pen name?

> **Tips for Writer's Block:**
> - Creative writing exercises
> - Create an Author's Promise to clarify your direction
> - Keep writing

If you are dealing with content that is going to need a brown paper bag around the jacket or an expose because you are a whistleblower, writing a manuscript that might jeopardize your employment, then yes, perhaps the situation warrants a pen name. Another case where using a pen name arises is when an author has books in several genres, and the agents and publishers are concerned about confusing the reader. Lastly, we have the rare situation where an author is successful in one genre and wants to explore another without repercussions or prejudice.

J.K. Rowling used a pen name for her first adult novel, *The Cuckoo's Calling*, and admitted she wanted to know if her writing in an adult genre was good enough to sell on its own, without her name as the calling card. Ann Rice and Stephen King are authors who have other pen names in multiple genres.

I had to explore this possibility when I branched out from non-fiction, having several heated discussions with my non-fiction agent as well as Peter and later a movie producer who had optioned two of my films. The bottom line is this: **conventional thinking by agents and editors is that an author won't have credibility if he/she jumps from one genre to another**. The reader will be confused and instead of lifting the book sales across the author's library, sales will drop, because readers will think that an author is trying to be all things to all people.

When I heard this, I immediately thought of Cher. Remember when she decided she wanted to act in addition to sing? She was skewered in the press and derided by the media before she starred in *Silkwood*. She proved everyone wrong by winning an Oscar. A reporter asked about her fearlessness [in trying something new] and she responded with a statement I have recalled time and again over the years.

"When I was in my twenties and thirties, I cared too much (about what people thought) and it affected me. Now in my fifties, I realize I wasted nearly three decades caring at all."

This became my battle cry and I refused to use a pen name.

Readers aren't stupid—and as a reader myself, I can clearly see when an author is branching out and I'm usually willing to give that author a shot. If the product was quality before, the first attempt in a new genre may not be perfect, but he/she will eventually get there.

A part of my philosophy was (and is) that the rising tide eventually floats all boats, and that some amount of crossover was eventually going to happen. A professional buying a business book certainly has hobbies and interests outside the office. That person might read action adventure or women's general interest and many other genres. We are multi-faceted beings, and to suggest that authors can only write on one topic is like telling an actor to be in only a certain type of movie. Sure, we like to watch our favorite star in a particular genre but it doesn't mean that actor will fail in another.

During this time, I will admit that everyone around me told me I was wrong with the lone exception of my husband. *Everyone.* His go-to-phrase was invariably: keep writing. Build your library. Don't worry about your pen name right now, because if you don't write good quality material, it won't matter anyway.

Bringing your Book to Market

CHAPTER HIGHLIGHTS

- *Print vs. digital*
- *Turning your book to other media*
- *Covers*

There's almost no author alive who isn't weathering the tumultuous changes in the publishing industry.

M.J. Rose

Millions of books are sold every year. If they weren't, publishers would close shop. While the overall numbers of certain formats are on the decline, book sales actually increase in times of a downturn or recession. Authors who want their books to stand the test of time are always interested in this type of data.

So was I, five years ago, when I was approached to write a

cookbook. The acquiring editor, from a mainstream house made an appealing case for why I should create a cookbook. I "had a name and a following," she told me. She saw I liked to blog about the food I made for family and entertaining, so it was "a perfect, complimentary match" with her publishing house that happened to boast quite a few celebrity chefs.

Although I was flattered, a cookbook was not, and still isn't, my area of focus. I certainly don't see myself as the next Ree Drummond with a cooking show or a life focused around food. Unconvinced, I inquired about the potential sales in an economic downturn.

"Oh, that's not an issue," the editor responded. "Two types of books are recession proof—romance novels and cookbooks." That was news to me, and she went one step further. "Depressed readers want to eat and escape, and those two categories fill the void." The message was loud and clear. Books provide repeat pleasure for a lower cost than going to the movies or out to eat.

It's tidbits like this that aren't found in books on finding an agent or how to market your self-published novel. Another one? **Forty percent of book buyers in the contemporary women's fiction market are men** (as told to me by a Barnes and Nobles marketing executive). It's because 1) men want to know what women are thinking and how they think, 2) men are interested in knowing what to do in and out of the bedroom to improve their relationship, and 3) they are looking for ideas on what to purchase for their significant other (or a person of interest).

With this in mind, I started to pay extra attention to the little things in my books that appealed to me but perhaps less so to a male reader. One specific example was a comment from a male reader who found me on Instagram, read three books and provided me feedback.

"I didn't mind the detailed description of the clothes in the beginning, but after a while, it was just enough to say black leather jacket, rather than delve into the collar type." Taking this comment as an author-improvement exercise, I re-read the two books and could see exactly what he meant. I adapted the writing in the next book I wrote, and after reading it, he remarked it was a better read.

Question 24: Do readers today still buy print copies or is it all digital?

Book purchasing trends vary with the category. According to my marketing specialist friend, "the industry" numbers, shared only within the publishing houses themselves, are the following:

- **Romance novels sell more eBooks than printed versions.**

This is because females in this genre are voracious readers, completing an average of 3 eBooks a week (this increases to 5 over the holidays and late summer). The Romance Writers of America site has dozens of statistics on the ages, media formats, preferences and buying habits of romance readers, and states that more printed books are purchased than eBooks. This contradicts every editor at the major houses I've spoken with, who tell me otherwise. Further, these same editors state that men will purchase the eBooks as well because "no-one will see the book jacket cover."

The only way I can reconcile this contradiction, and not get into a fight with the RWA, is to recognize that publishers have the actual buying information to back up this claim. I would also note that the RWA site continually references reader surveys and 'according to readers,' which suggests that their data comes from reader responses and not hard data.

- **Suspense, sci-fi and action adventure sell more printed versions.**

Buyers in this category are dominantly male and prefer reading a paperback or hardcover version by a margin of 70/30. Of these sales, nearly half the buyers will also purchase the eBook version of the same hard copy they just bought!

- **Non-fiction trade sell more printed versions in hardbound than any other category save cookbooks.**

Trade books are typically used for reference, the reader often making notes on the pages. Trade books also have a longer shelf-life, five years on average. Readers are willing to spend more on a book that will stand the test of time. **Non-fiction, trade sell first in printed version but the majority of readers also purchase the eBook version** of the same book.

This is a data point I love! In my three non-fiction books, the reports generated do indicate a strong correlation between print purchases and eBook purchases. That said, I will point out that my pricing strategy makes it less painful to purchase the eBook if the print book has already been purchased. To be specific, I made it between $2.99-.99 or free in some cases.

Question 25: Do readers have a preference for what format you choose in which to publish your book?

I'm going to answer this by relating a discussion that's been on-going amongst my contacts in the publishing industry. It relates to pricing and reader thresholds, and how the two influence reader preference and purchasing patterns.

When it comes to digital versus print, we can thank the dearly departed Steve Jobs for putting eBooks on the map. Apple artificially kept the price of the eBooks down, driving up the demand for both the digital versions but also the eBook reader devices. During this time, the number of eBooks sold tripled each year and the demise of the print book was predicted.

Sales of trade eBooks skyrocketed because business books are read by individuals on the go, and business travelers don't have the desire to carry pounds of books in their carry-on a plane. I know one human resource professional who has 500 business and non-fiction titles on her Nook.

That trend changed after Apple was sued and found guilty of price collusion. Fines were assessed and price of eBooks went back up, either to the same price as a print version or a bit lower. A few publishers have a policy that the eBook and the paperback are the same price, particularly with non-fiction books, such as trade, but also biographies, autobiographies and reference titles such as cookbooks. However, **on average, the price of an eBook is about 30% lower than the paperback version of the same title.**

Beyond pricing, reader preference

"Ultimately, it depends on the reader and the genre," said a publishing marketing specialist.

After asking this question for years now, I've found that **individuals over the age of fifty say they want a hard copy nearly 100% of the time. Those under thirty prefer to read an eBook on a device.** Generally, fiction is purchased by the recreational reader who wants the touch and feel of paper while sitting on the beach or lounging in the bathtub (the exception, as was stated earlier, is romance).

> Give your readers options for reading your work. Don't force the reader into your preferred format or device. Try to align it with the genre if at all possible. It could make all the difference in the world.

What should you do then? Offer the reader both formats, if you can afford it. Today, most publishers offer a choice of print and eBook and make them available across platforms (e.g. Amazon, B & N, Kobo etc.). The majority of self-published authors (over fifty-percent) begin by publishing their first book as an eBook. And it's not surprising. The ease and cost make it an appealing first path.

Question 26: What's the best way to bring my book to market?

1. **How old and patient are you?**

If you are forty, do you have the patience to wait a year to get an agent who will pitch your book and then wait another 3-6 months for a response from the publisher? (This assumes the agent takes your manuscript without any changes, and that's happened to me four times in thirteen books).

Then you must ask yourself if you are willing to wait another four years to receive your first royalty check, assuming you receive a publishing contract straight out of the gate, the editorial process goes without a hiccup and your book hits the shelves. At this point, you'd be forty-five and then the success of the book isn't guaranteed.

I know a British writer of fiction who has just turned forty-one, and after doing the math himself, he took the route of self-publishing, hoping the book would sell well enough to eventually help him get an agent. Because he's had minimal sales, he's learned that the book "isn't quite good enough" to be picked up, so he's going to hire a professional editor, upgrade the book and then go out again to agents and publishers.

2. Are you well organized and willing to spend a few thousand dollars on self-publishing?

Within self-publishing, many routes to market exist. I've observed the key to success in getting a book on the market comes down to organizational and project management capabilities and money. With enough money, almost anything can be accomplished, but who among us has limitless funds?

As you consider Table 5, take an honest assessment of your own strengths and weaknesses. I know a billionaire who wanted to publish his own book and so he hired a project manager, rather than go with one of the mainstream publishing houses. His focus came down to control: he wasn't going to have someone else dictate his story. His total out of pocket cost: $15,000. Another self-published author spent $1,200, paid CreateSpace (Amazon's imprint) to handle the cover and book formatting, but he skipped hiring an editor. In both cases, the book sales were low but higher than the national average. Specifically, the billionaire's book has sold 1,250 copies to date (and the project manager told me it was mostly due to his network of friends) and the independent author sold 600, which just about covered the cost of producing the book.

3. **Are you motivated by the notion of having your book on the shelf at your local bookstore and supermarket or is the money more important?**

If you fall into the former category, then your approach might be the traditional route of finding an agent and a mainstream publisher. I went that route with my first book and yes, it was wonderful to walk into bookstores and pick out my book. It was years before my ego shrunk in size and I was more focused on getting my books to market fast (six months versus two or more years) and making money even faster (a twenty-four hour period versus four years).

If you fall somewhere in the middle on one or all of these questions, then take a look at the options before you, because authors have plenty.

Table 5. Publishing options

Route	Requirements	Notes
Mainstream (Traditional) **Publisher**	An Agent	Non-fiction trade requires a proposal with an outline. Fiction requires the entire book. The exception to this is Children's books that require an illustrator, which is typically provided by the publisher.
Independent Publisher (formerly called vanity)	Money. Ranges from $10-20,000	You write the manuscript and they do the rest, including marketing and promotion. Some are more reputable and expensive than others.
eBook Publisher- type 1- "mainstream" type 2- "independent" type 3- "platform"	None-they pay you You pay them Free upfront- rev share model	An eBook publisher is interesting because **Type 1** provides a modest advance ($1,250 up to $2,500) but its exclusive (only available) through their channels. **Type 2** requires you pay them, but it's non-exclusive, and you are free to do other formats. **Type 3** is very popular because you distribute your books electronically on multiple sites and pay a flat percentage of the royalty. Draft2Digital is an example. D2D also provides free conversions for your eBook (epub, mobi) without requiring you to use their services (bonus!).
Self-publish houses	$0-3,500	Authors House, Dog Ear, Donovan—the difference from the Independent is the biggie-the marketing cost is separated out. So, on the surface, it is much cheaper, but the book gets no marketing. That is priced out separately, so either way, the author pays for the marketing, up front as in the independent route or at the end, in this model.
Self-publish (Publish on Demand, or **POD**)	Your time and money	CreateSpace (owned by Amazon) is the platform for more than 40% of all POD books. Barnes & Noble's Nook imprint is a close second and pays higher royalties.
Podcasts, audible books	Your time and money	Creating the audio & setting up a channel or a distribution deal for the books requires a degree of technical competence and audio skills. Hiring this out is worth it for the professionalism.

Question 27: I've listened to a lot of audible books, but for self-published authors, this seems cost prohibitive. Do I have alternatives?

The rising trend in the last forty-eight months is authors

experimenting with audible versions of their book. The most common version of this seem to be podcast/release per chapter. I've not done this myself, and for very specific reasons which I detail in the sales and promotion section, but I have spoken with authors who are using this as a preferred channel. I've also talked with, and interviewed, some of the voice professionals author hire.

The cost of the voice over professional is calculated by the word or the page count, but the average is about $35/hour. It takes about eight hours of reading to edit down a 350-page book into roughly four-five hours of podcasts. For longer books, the professionals charge a flat fee, and this is based upon the experience/resume of the voice professional. The fees I've seen start at $400 on up to about $800. Top talent, e.g. recognized celebrities, starts around $1,200 and goes up from there.

Regarding the technical acumen required for podcasts, this is a barrier for many authors. Let's assume you have a great voice and can read your own book. You need a quality sound system (a few hundred dollars for a good microphone, a room that doesn't echo and editing equipment). You then need to lead in and exit music. The best-selling chapter podcasts are less than 3 minutes in length. Most chapters are longer than that, so what does an author do? Edits the chapter down prior to reading the book. This is where the real talent comes into play, and it's not usually done by the author. Finally, posting, promoting and managing the podcast is required to make listeners aware of it.

Question 28: What about selling my chapters of the book on the way to a completed manuscript?

The answer I always give involves Stephen King and his experience with selling his books chapter by chapter back in 2000. It failed.

Tired with the slow-boat-to-China publishing model of manuscript to finished product and the one-book-a-year model, King experimented with offering a pay-per-chapter model for new material. He learned (and shared with the industry) that readers wanted free chapters and were unwilling to pay per chapter. So, what did he do? Went back to selling completed books at regular prices and the sales were steady and consistent.

Akin to this was a model that sprouted up around 2008-9, which was the bait-and-bill model used by a number of authors. The idea was to offer "free" chapters (delivered electronically). The reader was then billed at the end of the book. It was a nasty surprise and generated a lot of negative feelings towards authors.

Today, publishers and authors are still quick to reference both these events, with the final comment always something like: If Stephen King couldn't do it, nobody can.

It's still probably true.

Question 29: I don't understand why the routes to market take so long. What's involved and what are reasonable expectations?

Since I've gone through that cycle for a mainstream publisher in Chapter 1, I'll take you through the steps involved with a self-publish model.

The following timeline with steps pre-supposes you have already had your manuscript edited and proofed. It has been returned to you from the last proofreader and you are now going to take it forward yourself.

Having used CreateSpace (Amazon), Nook Print Press (Barnes & Noble) and others, I've found the average time from layout to a final proof product is on average ten days. The difference boils down to the complexity in the formatting and how this renders when the book is printed. Also, I've discovered that no matter how many times a book has been through a proofreader, errors always appear in the printed version. This is not just with self-published books. With McGraw-Hill, my title went through five editing rounds, and still, errors were found within the book.

Overlapping edits are part of the cause of this problem.

About book nine, I implemented a "final" round of proofreading that's done on the proof version of a printed book. It's simply easier to catch errors in a printed version. This may entail two rounds, one with the changes, then another proof copy, a second proofer to ensure the version is error free. And even then, readers will catch an error here and there.

Table 6. Self-publishing timeline

Activity	Length	Notes
Layout	3-5 days	Using the layout template provided by the platform you choose (e.g. CreateSpace, B & N etc.). Modify according to the style and format of the book (trade vs fiction) Upload the formatted book for approval
Cover	Simultaneous	Upload the formatted cover for approval Option to use a template or designer
Review on-line version	1 day (hours)	Make changes as necessary to the inside and cover
Order proof copy	2-10 days	CreateSpace delivers a 2-day proof whereas Nook Press is 7-10 days.

Once you receive the proof copy of the printed version, you inspect it from cover to cover, and you may even find new edits you'd like to make. Plan for two weeks for another review cycle.

During this time, you set up the marketing page(s) associated with the book as well as the eBook version. In order to capture all of the necessary information, such as the ISBN(s) for each version of the book, page count and type of paper, the size of the book and other details, this is a good time to create a master spreadsheet. It will make it easy when you start to market your book across on-line sites, and help ensure the content is consistent and accurate.

This is what a basic "book product line" for a single book would look like.

Table 7. eBook imprints and offerings

Entity	eBook imprint	Paperback	Hardcover
Amazon	Amazon Kindle	CreateSpace	Not offered
B & N	Nook Press	Print Nook Press	Print Nook Press
Kobo/iTunes, Tolino, Draft to Digital	**Same as previous**	N/A	N/A

Question 30: What's the best strategy to get my book out to the majority of readers?

In the US, Amazon and B & N serve over eighty percent of the on-line market. Some figures are higher than that, but it's generally accepted if you have books on both channels, you are going for the optimum exposure.

Referring to the previous table, this means you have five

offerings for a single book: two eBooks and three print formats, two paperback and one hardbound. A sixth if you elect hardbound with a flap. It is up to you to determine the best format for your genre.

Question 31: What's the most profitable way to get my book out there if I'm self-publishing? In other words, where will I make the most money?

Barnes & Noble (via Print Nook Press) provides the highest royalty rate for a non-exclusive distribution. Amazon provides a 70% royalty rate but the book must be exclusive to Amazon for a period of time (90 days minimum) and then more if you want to continue making the 70% royalty. All this fine print can be confusing, and fortunately, I had my trusty helper go through the financial implications (otherwise known as my husband). It helps he has a finance background, and here's what we learned through trial and error—(I must say he predicted this would be the case, even before he ran the numbers).

Volume over royalty

When I first launched with Amazon, I thought "They are the largest in the country and I want the most royalty, so of course I'll sign an exclusive." For a year or more, I stayed exclusively with Amazon. Then I started reading the reports about B & N holding sixty percent of the US sales for eBooks. I was astounded, and then I read more about their market of printed books. Because they have hardcover (and Amazon doesn't), B & N has a higher market number than Amazon.

It occurred to me that I was missing a huge market of potential readers, so I went back and changed all my accounts with Amazon to a 35% royalty rate and a non-exclusive status.

Then the real work began. It took me the entire summer of 2017 to create new interiors and have the covers modified for the Print Nook Press and Nook Press requirements. This was a total of 28 new versions of my existing books. I cover the tips for managing and delivering a library to market later, but the effort was worth it. While my royalty per book was significantly lower, the volume of sales skyrocketed and I kicked myself for not making that change several years earlier.

Question 32: How much money can I make self-publishing?

Like so many of the previous questions, the answer depends on many variables: the format, page count, paper type and most of all, the list price. I learned through trial and error that the best size for highest profits is 6 x 9, and if I use slimmer margins on either side, the page count is lower. The following model explains my exact royalties.

Table 8. Royalty comparison CreateSpace vs Nook

	Sue Kim	TOE	ACD	Chambers
Page count	311	211	365	354
Book size	5.5 X 8.5	5.5 X 8.5	6 X 9	5.25 X 8.5
Amazon eBook	**List:** $12.99 **Royalty: $4.55**	**List:** $12.99 **Royalty: $4.55**	**List:** $6.99 **Royalty: $2.45**	**List:** $6.99 **Royalty: $2.80**
Amazon paperback	**List:** $14.95 **Royalty: $4.24**	**List:** $14.95 **Royalty: $3.35**	**List:** $14.95 **Royalty: $3.35**	**List:** $15.95 **Royalty: $3.44**
B & N eBook	N/A	**List:** $6.99 **Royalty: $4.54**	**List:** $6.99 **Royalty: $4.54**	**List:** $6.99 **Royalty: $4.54**
B & N paperback	**List:** $14.95 **Royalty: $3.52**	**List:** $12.95 **Royalty: $3.64**	**List:** $15.95 **Royalty: $3.64**	**List:** $15.95 **Royalty: $1.94**
B & N hardcover	**List:** $22.95 **Royalty:** $3.08	**List:** $19.95 **Royalty: $2.65**	N/A	**List:** $19.95 **Royalty: $2.60**

Sue Kim and *The Overlooked Expert* (TOE) are non-fiction. *A Convenient Date* (ACD) and *Chambers* are fiction in the women's general interest and action-adventure genres respectively.

*Note on the pricing table: that's a point in time and I'm fluctuating the prices every so often depending on the time of year. E.g. for Christmas, the price of my books a dollar or so. But at the time of this writing, what's in the table are the prices and royalties.

Question 33: Is my finished manuscript suited for a made-for-tv movie, Netflix or HBO?

Depending on your genre, the answer is a definite yes. **Romance, Christian or women's contemporary fiction are the most transferrable genres to television because production costs are low**. There are no explosions like an action/suspense/thriller genre, nor is there a high pay scale required by a drama requiring brand-name actors. Not to demean those three categories (how could I? I write in two of them), but the scenes (sets) and nature of the topic typically make it a lower cost effort.

"Great!" you say, already thinking your manuscript might have the luck of Danielle Steele's many made-for-television movies. I encourage you to pursue this path as long as you understand the typical compensation structure.

Rights and returns

The major networks purchase the rights to your manuscript, make the made-for-tv movie, and you receive royalties every time the show airs. If you have a following, or have made a name for yourself, you may be able to negotiate a percentage of the advertising revenue, which is where all the real money is at. This is how actors and writers who haven't been in a production for years still appear on the annual "money-maker's" list. Their agent inserted a line for a percentage of the advertising revenue on top of the royalty for acting. Authors don't always have this same type of pull, but it never hurts to try. That said, even if you don't get it, your name is on the credit as "based on the book by…" which helps create awareness for your other books and increases the money you'll hopefully be paid for your next made-for-tv project.

> The best way to make money from the small screen is to have a book that gets picked up by a network television station, or a cable network that will pay residuals.

Flat fees

HBO and cable companies are a different story altogether. During my days as a consultant, I was working with a C-level executive at HBO (who wishes to remain anonymous), and over a period of time, we became good close enough that I asked him about offering up one of my books to HBO.

"Oh, no, you don't ever want to do that," he said, his vehemence taking me by surprise. He explained how HBO and other cable companies in general work. "We are the most profitable cable company because we are really cheap." He went on to explain HBO's model.

HBO purchases "the work" from the author, be it a script or manuscript. The average price is a $60,000, flat fee. No residuals, no royalties and it's rebranded an "HBO Original." While the writers are listed in the credits, it's not with the tagline "based upon" your work.

You will notice that the really big-name actors received a "produced by" or "created by" because this is a draw for talent. "But these are the exceptions," he emphasized. "The actual author is submerged by the HBO brand."

That means the author—you or I—are essentially work-for-hire. He described individuals (authors) who live in New York or elsewhere around the world who make a fine living cranking out screenplays for HBO at sixty-thousand each. If one can write fast and the pieces are picked up, it's good money. On the other hand, it's per project, and there is no guarantee an author will ever have more than one purchased.

He did acknowledge that a few of the other cable companies are more generous than HBO, but his executive team believes that their compensation is fair for the right type of writer.

"We have the best name in the business. A lot of writers want to work with us, but not the serious authors." Note that he made the distinction between writer and author. An author produces novels, while a writer produces television or cable shows.

Question 34: Do covers really sell a book?

"Purchasing a book is just like purchasing a wine," one acquisitions editor said to me. "The decision is made in less than a minute and is largely based on the cover."

That line has been repeated by many of my industry friends, but I must say, I don't believe it---entirely. I'm a reader, and as much as I like a cover, I'm going to read the text on the back and maybe a review or two—just enough to get a sense of the plot. My money matters too much to spend even five bucks based solely on the color scheme or picture. And if the cover is amateurish or from a template, then the odds I will purchase the book plummets. **In other words, the quality of the book cover is representative of what's inside.**

You can't go wrong if you create a cover that:

1. fits the genre
2. captures the attention of the consumer and
3. portrays a sense of excitement and interest.

While the initial impression encourages the consumer to investigate further, the real focus should be on word of mouth and reviews. Studies have shown that the number one influence for book purchases is referrals from a trusted source. That's why reviews are so critical to book sales, and why aspiring authors are willing to do just about anything for a good one.

Question 35: If I write Women's Romance, do I need to have a nearly naked man on the cover?

No, but you do need to match or align the content with the cover. A Harvard business study shows that a person makes up his/her own mind about a product or person in 3 seconds or less. Those three seconds will cause the consumer to make a flash decision about whether to learn more or not. Once the purchase has been made, the reader will need to have his or her initial expectations met by the content. When it doesn't, you have lost the trust of the reader. When the inside of a book hasn't matched the outside, it takes me a very long time to buy another book from the author, and usually will only do so if a friend has read it and provided a good report.

Question 36: How do I compare agents?

Initially, you are going to go after an agent who specializes in your genre, who is accepting new authors and has a passion for your project. Call it the greed factor or simple economics, agents have to eat, and that can only happen if they sell manuscripts to publishers. As a result, they are always on the look-out for the "next big thing." This means that unless an agent has a full list of bestselling authors, they are going to accept submissions or inquiries in their identified areas of interest.

One way of comparing agents is the contract, but this is a myopic view of things since agent contracts are nearly identical. With my first agent, Matt Wagner, the relationship was straightforward, easy and professional.

The fiction world has been a bit bumpier, and as I've learned the hard way, the most important aspect of the agent-author relationship is the personal connection. It's like any long-term relationship--there will be ups and downs involving hard conversations and victories. You have to treat it with the same level of respect and consideration you apply to other important relationships.

- Do you get along?
- Is your relationship genuine and real?

- Do you get the time and attention you require, but also honest feedback?
- Does the agent actually care? And by this, I mean two things: a) have they read your work and b) have they given you feedback on how to improve?

A tale of two agents

I'll give two different examples of fiction agents: one agent just sat back and road the wave while another worked hard on my behalf, fired me, then re-signed me, making me a better author in the end.

The first agent I'll call Mary. She was in her late twenties, serving as an agent with a top firm in New York. One editor I worked with told me Mary had a discerning eye and "discovered" two different, unpublished authors and then worked hard to get each a publishing deal. Both shot up the *New York Times* Bestseller list.

I was recommended to Mary by an editor who knew the boss of the literary agency Mary worked for. I spoke with Mary, thought her to be energetic, enthusiastic, and most of all, eager. Young agents are the best (or so I was told) because they are "hungry."

For her part, she certainly expressed an eagerness to represent me. I'd just inked the movie option deal for *Chambers* and she had a sure-fire winner on her hands. She created a brochure to pitched Chambers at the Frankfurt Book Fair, where she closed three foreign publishing deals on my behalf and had eight other foreign publishers waiting in the wings for when the movie went into production.

Then she went dark. By that, I mean, pitch black. The initial contracts were done and so was she. For months, I'd call to ask about status, feedback or anything else, and got nothing. As you can imagine, it was rational to seek insight when not a single US publisher was making me an offer after I had a movie deal in hand and three foreign contracts. When she did finally get on the phone she had no answers.

"What did they think of the book?" I asked. She couldn't give me a response. "Well, are there things in the book that you would change? Or that I should consider for book two?" When she hemmed and hawed on that response, it didn't sit right. I went back to the editor who referred me to Mary and told her about the situation.

"I bet she never read it," my editor said. "How was that possible?" I inquired. "Happens all the time," she replied. Unwilling to believe that my agent had never even cracked open my book, I decided to test the theory. The next time we got in the phone, I asked Mary specific questions about the middle and ending, subtly enough where she wouldn't notice what I was doing, but worded in such a way that she couldn't avoid the question.

Ultimately, I decided to out her.

"You never read it, did you?" Only then did she acknowledge the truth. Needless to say, I ended the relationship shortly thereafter. She'd get paid on the contracts she'd finalized but nothing in the future. How could she possibly speak to a potential acquisition editor about the book (plotline or comparatives to competing books) if she'd never read the darn thing?

A stellar agent will care enough to read your work, give you critical feedback and kick your butt if that's what it takes to improve your chances of success.

Now compare this to my relationship with Peter Rubie. He took me on, read my manuscript from front to back and cared enough to give me incredible resources to improve my writing.

At first, it was *100 Most Common Mistake in First Time Authors* (which still sits on my shelf). Later, when I switched genres and had hit a plateau, he took the first twenty-five pages of my manuscript and gave me what's called a "hard-edit." It was redlined and marked up.

Given that Peter taught at NYU for ten years as an adjunct professor, I felt like I'd just benefited from a master's writing course. Last but not least, Peter cared enough to fire me as an author when, after nearly five years together, he could no longer do anything for me or I him. I agreed, went on my way, spent three more years developing my skillset, then came back to him when I believed I'd improved. It was like auditioning for the starring role all over again.

I thanked him, telling him he cared enough to kick my butt and do what was necessary for me to graduate to the next level. Peter then became my agent for both my non-fiction and fiction work, and still is today.

Question 37: How do I find and get in touch with an agent?

- **In trade magazines**. Read *PW* for the names of agents that represent authors in your genre. Be real about results. If they are getting mentioned in *PW*, they likely have a long client list and may not take on new authors.
- **By recommendation**. If you know anyone in the industry, ask for a recommendation. Be aware that the person making the connection will be putting his or her name on the line for you. Before I give a recommendation, I insist on reading the book and liking it enough before sending it on. If your friend or intermediary doesn't like your book, you need to try another route.
- **Solicitation from the agent website**. Search agent websites. Most, if not all, list whether or not they are accepting solicitations. You can go directly to agents through their contact information listed on the website or in the form.
- **List serves**. If you know an editor, or can get on an editorial list-serve, do this and ask for a recommendation for an agent in a specific genre.

You can also purchase a resource guide or list of agents. This was my approach as I contemplated writing NTPM. I went to the local bookstore and spent twenty bucks on the hard-bound copy. Today, the same list can be found online through a simple search.

Editing

CHAPTER HIGHLIGHTS

- *The role of editing*
- *Types of editor, costs and results*
- *Expectations based on publishing type*

To write is human, to edit is divine.

Stephen King

It takes a single word to explain why so many books don't sell, an aspiring author isn't accepted by an agent and a publisher will reject your book. It's called editing. In this chapter you are going to read a lot of cringe-worthy stories which are worth suffering through because you may learn what so many aspiring authors don't understand.

Question 38: Do I really need an editor?

Everyone needs an editor, and usually more than one kind. An editor helps shape or clarify the overarching theme(s) or subject(s) of the books, increases the pacing, improves the flow, catches slow sections, points out inconsistencies and so forth. Other editors step in at different points in the process to further improve the manuscript. If you ever question the value of an editor, turn to the acknowledgments/thanks page of a book. The first person named is invariably the editor, not the agent, who is a close second. Without a good product, there is no book and hence no sales, leaving the agent without a job. Find the right editor and trust the opinions put forth.

The author's excuse: "I'm a writer not an editor." Your passion may be to write, but your work is going to be to edit. You can take the easy path and hire others, but you will never improve your writing if you don't learn how to edit.

Question 39: As the author, how much work am I expected to do when it comes to editing?

A lot, and that doesn't apply just to self-publishing. Whether you have been picked up by a mainstream publisher, or are paying to bring your book to market, the top line of editing—where it counts the most—can usually only be accomplished by the author. The lone exception to this is where you have hired a contractor who actually writes the manuscript. This is often referred to as a ghost writer who is hired at the outset of the project.

Question 40: What are the circumstances where I'd hire a contract writer?

When you are out of options.

- **Your manuscript is rejected.**

I shared an agent with one author who submitted a non-fiction book that was rejected twice. My agent confided he feared the author would be forced to hire a contractor if the manuscript already under contract was rejected a third time. Sure enough, it was rejected, the deadline was looming and the entire contract was in jeopardy. Without any other options, the author spent nearly five thousand dollars for an expert to help complete the manuscript.

- **You overcommitted.**

In fiction, many authors live on the advances of books not yet written. This encourages the author to commit to aggressive schedules (think a book submitted every three or four months). It seems impossible, but many authors do it, leaving no leeway for life interruptions. When delays occur and the author is in a bind, a contractor is hired.

- **You have lost interest or simply aren't good at it.**

I've seen an author of non-fiction branch out into cookbooks (because he loved cooking) only to find that his recipes didn't translate to great pictures, prose was choppy and the process of refining the flow was making him increasingly angry. He had the choice to give the advance money back or figure it out. His agent located a chef who took on the project for a fee, was acknowledged as an "inspiration" in the back matter, but essentially was the true brain behind the cookbook.

Question 41: If I have hired an independent publisher, and need to hire a contractor, who pays, me or the publisher?

I'll refer you back to the example of the billionaire who paid about $15,000 to have his book written and published. He started writing it, ran out of time and hired a contractor. The independent publisher didn't know or care who wrote the submitted manuscript: the first draft required changes and someone had to do it. The feedback was provided in an editorial letter (which was proceeded by a rather intense conversation between the project manager at the publishing house and the contractor). The contractor made the suggested/required changes and submitted the rewrite.

Whether you do it yourself or you hire it out, the top line changes to the manuscript will be done by the author, not the publishing house.

Question 42: I have an agent but not a publishing deal. Am I expected to get my manuscript professionally edited before submitting it to the agent?

Usually, because the competition for a book deal is so fierce, you can't submit a less than great product. A first time writer has to be better than an established one.

The details, then, depend on how much time and money you

have as well as your risk factor. Are you willing to risk having your agent read the book, reject it, send it back to you for a rewrite, then expect him or her to read again? This will cost you six months, and that's if—a big if—your agent will prioritize the time to reread the new version, or if you will get backlogged. Good agents typically have a backlog of 3 months at least. If you follow the above process, you have just lost nine months.

Let's take it from another angle, one that's based in reality. Many agents don't read your manuscript at all. When they don't read your book (some perhaps but not all) they will send it out "blind," as it's called. In some cases, the manuscript is in good shape (or good enough) and the agent gets lucky. Otherwise, the publisher rejects the manuscript and rarely gives a reason, other than perhaps "it needs more work." The agent has technically done their job but the author has no more insight as to what *more work* actually means.

Now I know you are thinking about Stephenie Meyer, who sent her unrepresented manuscript to nearly ninety acquisition editors. There are a few other examples of authors who were persistent and got a great publishing deal but not many. I think Amanda Hawking is a better example. She self-published her eBooks and built a library of work, eventually earning tens of thousands of dollars a month. Sales caught the attention of agents and publishers, and she got a seven-figure deal with a publishing house (I will refer back to her story later). Did she use an editor? Absolutely, before her work went up for sale.

Ultimately, presenting the best possible book to your agent

and publisher improves the chances it will be accepted.

Testing out your book with a reader

Not long after *Chambers* was optioned, I was interviewed by a reporter from a local paper. He came to the house, took some pictures, asked a lot of questions, wrote a nice article and a few months later called me for advice. He'd written a novel, about 750 pages and asked if I'd read it. I did and gave him my honest feedback. The idea was original, the characters solid and pacing fair. But it was far too long, convoluted and confusing in certain areas, had too many characters and should be split into three books or at least rewritten with that in mind.

> The desired deal happened for two reasons: a professional editor and the right attitude and willingness of the author to adapt and learn.

"But," I warned, "I'm not a professional editor in this area, only a reader. So, hear my comments with that in mind." I take him if he had the money and interest in working with a professional and he jumped at the chance. After referring him to an editor who works in his genre (suspense/thriller) he hired her, rewrote the manuscript, got an agent and a deal! (FYI, it cost him $250).

Contrast that to another experience that followed within months. Another aspiring author was referred to me by a local bookstore owner, Jane. One day I'm in Jane's store for a book signing event, she asks me for a favor.

"I have this woman who is a good customer, but she keeps pestering me about her book and I hope you can help me out." Jane requested I read the manuscript and give feedback. "It's not my genre or style, and I couldn't get past the first twenty pages," she admitted. Thinking that it would be as good as the last experience I'd had with the young reporter, I readily agreed.

The woman, whom I'll call Sharon, sent me her printed manuscript and I began reading. I still remember spending several afternoons struggling through this book. The basic premise upon which the book was based and the way she pulled it off, was simply amazing. It is one of two books I've ever read by a non-published author that I told my husband, "I wish I'd come up with this idea."

Unfortunately, that was the only thing I could recommend about the book—the idea. At the highest level, the story line went back and forth and it wasn't structurally sound. Because the story lacked basic structure, it was hard to keep the plot straight and caused me to put down the manuscript multiple times so I could clear my head and lower my frustration level. The worst offense wasn't the bad structure or the writing, both of which are correctable with a good editor and time. It was the characters. The entire book had a flavor of bitterness that I'd not read before. Still, when I finished, I was absolutely sure it was correctable with strong editing. Jane thanked me profusely, sure Sharon would take my feedback to heart. In my email to Sharon, I applauded the strong points of the book and provided my overarching thoughts on how an editor could better her manuscript. Sharon never responded. Sometime later, I was at the bookstore and caught up with Jane. She shook her head and frowned.

"Sharon based the lead character on herself and doesn't believe the book needs to be changed at all. She likes it the way it is."

As far as either Jane or I know, the book is still the way it was then—unchanged and on her computer.

Question 43: Where do you find a good editor?

You get a referral from a trusted and proven source in the industry if possible.

The first editor I used was Pam Liflander, who was recommended to me by non-fiction editor, Matt Wagner, from Waterside Communications (he's since left and started his own agency). To provide the context, I had my own issues writing my first non-fiction trade book, *Navigating the Partnership Maze*. I was accustomed to using a third or first person informal voice, and it wasn't pointed out to me by the acquisition editor that I needed to write the manuscript in third-person formal. Wups. As a result, my first manuscript was rejected and I was beside myself. Not only that, but my editor had issues with the book's overall organization. She didn't like it, suggesting the flow didn't work for her.

> Reedsy is a great site that many of my editorial contacts use to find skill professionals when they are in tight spots (think strategic, copy, line or proofreaders). If it's good enough for them it may work for you.

"But it conforms to the outline we agreed upon," I said logically. It didn't matter, she wanted a change. I did what all authors do: I went right back to Matt Wagner, my non-fiction agent who had sold the deal to McGraw-Hill, honestly telling him I had no idea what to do and how to start. In so many words, Matt said fix it, so I tried another response, "If I knew how to fix it, I'd do it myself."

Pam Liflander came highly recommended from Matt because she had been on both sides of the publishing world. First as a successful acquisitions editor at several major houses in New York. When she left to raise a family, she continued editing for special projects, and this morphed into ghost writing for NYT bestselling authors of non-fiction. When I met her, she had her hands full ghost writing and editing, and was also embarking on writing under her own name.

"Are you willing to do what it takes to get this manuscript in shape?" Absolutely, I replied. "It means you will need to rewrite every sentence of the entire book." I didn't even pause before affirming my commitment. She told me she'd send me the contract, but I could still back out of the project after she edited the first fifty pages.

"Why would I do that?" I inquired.

"Most authors either don't want to put in the work to make the manuscript right or they reject the changes that are suggested."

Sure enough, the first fifty pages I received was blood red with edits, and that was after I made the structural changes to get the flow going. And yet I stuck with her and got my book published.

Question 44: What do I look for in an editor/what questions do I ask?

- **Experience as an editor**

Pam had been an acquisitions editor for not just one, but several major houses. She knows the criteria, standards and unwritten rules to get manuscripts through the editorial and marketing process.

- **Experience in your genre**

The formats, formulas and requirements vary dramatically from genre to genre. I had no idea just how much until after my first non-fiction book had been published. The floodgates opened and I suddenly found myself being asked for introductions to editors and agents from all sorts of aspiring authors. As the inquiries came in, I'd do my best to connect the aspiring author with the right editor. Rarely was I able to do so. Pam, for instance, doesn't have experience in children's books but knows editors who do.

- **A track record of working with authors**

An editor may have the knowledge and skills but lack the interpersonal skills to work well with an author. Providing feedback is a delicate balance between honesty and diplomacy, both in writing and over the phone. I've had interactions where the phone conversation is agreeable, and I read the editorial letter which has a similar, upbeat tone. Then I'd read the chapter by chapter remarks and couldn't tell if my editor was grumpy, tired, or really, truly hated what I've put down on the paper.

You need to suss out the communication tone before you spend your money. If your editor can't convey direction in a way that's meaningful to you or if you're unable to hear it (for whatever reason), the project will fail and you will be without an improved manuscript and money.

Question 45: What should I expect to receive from an editor?

You and the editor define the deliverables in accordance with your needs and budget. Assuming you can't get an agent and you don't know why, you need help. In this case, you require three things:

1. A review of the entire book with feedback on what's right, wrong and in-between.
2. A chapter-by-chapter breakdown that support these points, but also tell you specifically what you need to do in order to make it the best possible product.
3. A way to manage the "next step," following your re-write.

In this situation, you should expect and ask for an Editorial Letter. This may be 1-5 pages explaining the editor's overall comments/concerns about the book. Separate from this letter, but still a part of the project (and under the same contract) will be a document that goes through each chapter. Together, this constitutes the project, in addition to a call or two with the editor to clarify certain points. My editors build in 2 hours of conversation because the second document is almost always 20-40 pages, depending on the length of the manuscript and the amount of changes required. If this runs over, you will be billed the additional hours at the end.

Question 46: Is there more than one editing round?

When I think of this type of editing, I look at it as a project with two parts: Part 1 is strategic editing and feedback. The interim step is you making the changes. Part 2 is the review and finalization of the manuscript. Part 2 is a separate contract with the same editor, wherein the book is re-read and checked for changes. Depending on the structure that works best for you, the editor and the changes to the manuscript, it can take several forms. If the book is in good shape overall, then you may submit only those areas that required a lot of revising. On the other hand, if the book needed a lot of changes, the entirety will be reviewed.

For my early books within the women's contemporary genre, I would actually call my editor to discuss plot resolution issues to ensure I was getting it right, then I'd proceed to revise the first five chapters or fifty pages. In other cases, the logical breaking point was 100 pages before I sent it off. Don't get caught up in the page count or chapter numbers. The focus should be on logical breaks for you and the editor to review and finalize.

Question 47: How long does this editing round take and how much does it cost?

Once again, this depends (don't you love that word by now)? The length of time is dependent on the volume and depth of changes, how long it takes you to suitably address each one and the back and forth between you and the editor. Remember, the editor has a schedule of other authors in the que, and you will be slotted in accordingly.

That said, I will tell you one of the reasons you are paying a lot of money is because the editor should be taking on only so many clients so they can give you a clear timeframe for editing your work.

To give you a rough idea of my history with strategic editors, it is best to break it down in a table. In the following table, I've listed the last eight books. It shows how much editing I required in the beginning and where my current needs stand.

Table 9. Strategic (top-line) editing cost and timeframes

Book	Edit round 1	Cost	Edit round 2	Cost
Chambers (YA)	3 months	$2,200	45 days	$1,800
Navigating the Maze (non-fiction)	2 months	$2,100	3 weeks	$900
A Convenient Date (women's fiction)	3.5 months	$2,100	6 weeks	$1,900
Made for Me (women's fiction)	2 months	$1,900	5 weeks	$1,600
Destined for You (women's fiction)	7 weeks	$1,350	4 weeks	$800
In a Moment (women's fiction)	0	0	3 weeks	$900
10th Edition Overlooked Expert (non-fiction)	0	0	0	0*
Author Straight Talk (non-fiction)	0	0	30 days	$850

*line editing proofing only- these costs are broken out in another table.

Question 48: How are the bills typically paid?

Fifty percent is due before the start of the project and the balance is due after the final product is completed. The final bill is provided after you have received the edited manuscript, and you've had the last conversation about the project with the editor.

When your editor says: "I'll be available to look at another copy just in case you aren't sure," that's translation for: you are really close to the edge here, and would be wise to have someone, anyone, look at this again before it goes off to layout.

Question 49: So, in theory, I'm going to actually improve my writing by hiring an editor?

Absolutely. Some people go to vocational training and sit in a classroom in order to practice a skill. Think of this as an investment in your future. I never went to graduate school. I consider the money I put towards the editing process my master's program. Table 9 is a list of books I wrote <u>after</u> I began using strategic editing because the ones I wrote prior to that I have put on a virtual shelf, and for good reason.

As Peter reflected after I'd written *In a Moment*, the biggest testament to my improved writing was the reduction in the amount or editorial work required by the editor.

"You didn't need the work and she knew it," Peter said.

Question 50: After the top-line, strategic editing, then what?

You have 2-4 more editing rounds to go, but don't freak out. Each one is necessary to improve your writing. For practical purposes, budget 2 weeks for each step, just to be on the safe side and use Table 10 as a guide.

If you are starting out, you should set your expectations that you will need one or all of the following editorial services: Copy editor, line editor and proof readers.

Table 10. Editorial steps, costs and tasks

Editor	When used	Cost	Source	Main tasks
Strategic editor	Completed manuscript (you have taken it as far as you can)	$95-$125/hour	Referral but can also be found on line	Structure, flow, concepts, characters
Line editor	After rewrites from the version 2 (above)	$45-$95/hour	Writer's forums or on-line sites	Editing at the chapter and paragraph level
Copy editor	After version 3 (above)	$45-$95/hour	Writer's forums or on-line sites	Line by line editing. Word choice, sentence phrasing
Proof reader 1	After version 4 (above) "pre-final" version	$15-$25/hour	On-line but also local resources like teachers and even readers	
Proof reader 2	After version 5 "final"	$15-$25/hour	Same as above	

Bringing a book to market is a lot of money for any publisher, especially if that publisher is you. Now that you are starting to get a handle on the costs (and we haven't gotten to covers, marketing and sales yet), you can see why publishers pay so little for advances in today's market. The reality is that money is a finite resource, and so is the time you spend editing. If you are forced to make a choice on where you spend your money, you must get the story arc, the flow, the pacing and the characters right. In other words, you absolutely make editing a priority, no ifs, ands, or buts. The cover, formatting and other elements will have to wait. Imagine the scenario: you are the reader who loved the cover and back-of-the-book write-up. You are two pages into it, and a sentence doesn't read right, and words are missing. The disappointment is heightened because of the expectations. Don't do that to your reader. Spend the money on editing.

> You have one chance to impress the acquisitions editor, or the reader. If you rush the process or skip over the essentials, you have broken the trust with the editor or reader who may or may not ever give your work another opportunity again.

Question 51: What's the difference between a line editor and a copy editor?

- **A line editor** is going to focus on the transitions between chapters, sections, paragraphs and sentences. The goal is to improve the flow of the narrative or topics. A line editor will also look at sentence structure to ensure it reads smoothly and logically.

One challenge you may have is that the editor's writing style won't necessarily be your writing style. You may have to contend with their choice of structure and style of writing. I've witnessed times where an author's voice was completely submerged due to a heavy-handed line editor and had to be re-written. So, talk to a prospective line editor and make sure they work to improve your words and writing style and not substitute it with their own.

➢ **A copy editor** is another level down, concentrating on the precise words you are using, looking for redundancy (the same word in two paragraphs apart), contradictions (blue on one page, purple on another), location names, spelling errors, and the like. Also, a copy editor is going to look at the formatting, the font, the indenting and other conventions (or styles) that you have chosen to use throughout the book in order to ensure consistency.

In my last non-fiction book, the 10th Anniversary Edition of *The Overlooked Expert*, the copy editor jokingly told me I must have recently gone through a divinely-inspired self-reflection period, because I'd used some variation of the word 'ascertain' more than ten times in the manuscript. I did a search and sure enough, I'd been in an ascertaining mode. My next step was to go through and change the words or sentences to make my point without being redundant. By the same token, I was mixing up fonts in certain call-outs and text boxes.

An editor might describe the former issue (overuse of a word) "lazy writing," because I'd unconsciously fallen back on a word that was comfortable. The latter problem was simply oversight. I thought was catching everything but wasn't. Thankfully, the copy editor caught both.

Question 52: Will I have a different experience with an independent publisher, whom I'm paying to do all this work for me?

I'm not going to comment on every independent publisher out there, especially because I've not personally used one. However, I know quite a few authors who have chosen to work with independent publishers. There are a few differences, but I'm not going to use names (again, because this is second hand). My goal is to provide pointers so you can select the right independent publisher for you.

- Have your assigned project manager give you specific examples of past projects, from the easiest to the hardest (e.g. the author submitted a manuscript that was very clean, almost pre-edited, to the other end where the manuscript was barely readable) and how they handled each incident.
- Understand in explicit terms what types of editing are provided, and what you, the author, should expect with each editor.
- Understand the names and general turn-around timeframe of the process.
- Be suspicious if several levels/roles are combined into one editor. A generalist is apt to make more mistakes.
- Pay close attention to the turnaround cycles—both on their side and yours. Is it realistic? What happens if an editor is sick? Do

they have a back-up?

- Can they point to other books that you can read, or other authors in your genre, who have had successes with this organization?
- One critical area is marketing and sales, especially for the independent publishers, but more on that in future chapters.

Question 53: What can I realistically expect from an external editorial process?

When you are paying professionals, you expect the final product to pop. Both with mainstream publishers and on my own, the final product(s) has met or surpassed my expectations. I'll give you an example where that wasn't the case, one I witnessed first-hand.

A business associate of mine in the financial industry had earned enough money to fund micro-businesses domestically and overseas. He wanted to share his financial advice and paid a consultant fifteen thousand dollars to write the book (as a ghost writer), and another twenty thousand to an independent house to bring it to market. It's perhaps 150 pages, the graphics are modest and the cover design okay. It didn't blow me away either positively or negatively. It was straight down the middle. The marketing and sales efforts didn't help sell enough copies to cover the production costs.

In reading a copy of the book (which he gave me), I was enlightened by the information but not compelled. As a consumer, I thought to myself: Did I change my habits as a result of reading the book? No. Did I look forward to sitting down and picking up the book? No, it felt like an obligation, not a choice. The ultimate litmus test: Did I recommend the book to a single person? No. I wanted to love the book when I picked it up, and with each page I turned, I hoped it would get better and, ultimately, I'd be satisfied, but I wasn't.

At the end of the day, the reason good editors within a publishing house are so highly prized is they have the ability to spot dead paragraphs, finetune the pacing of the storyline and improve the characters. If an editor is doing no more than pushing the project from one desk to another there is no value in the process at all, other than having a printed book on the shelf.

Question 54: How often should I expect to speak to my editor?

This is a very, yet vague question. Ultimately, it relies upon the type of house you are working with and the relationship that's been set up via the contract. You could call a consultant every day if you wanted to…you just have to pay for it.

On this topic, I'll differentiate between a project manager and an editor. The project manager has the overall responsibility for bringing your manuscript to market. It used to be that in the mainstream publishing world, the project manager actually was the editor, but today, the acquisitions editor is more administrative than hands-on. This person will guide you to and from the editors in the process, ensuring issues are resolved.

Daily interaction? No, only when it's near the end of the project.

Weekly calls? Usually around the planned milestones.

Question 55: Do I wait until the entire manuscript is done or send in chapters?

This depends on the established process of the publishing house and sometimes the type of work. For non-fiction, I've had different publishers request both—a completed manuscript or several chapters at a time. The larger the publisher, the greater the likelihood the complete manuscript will be requested. Fiction is almost always submitted in its entirety.

Question 56: If the proofreaders are so good, why do I still see errors in printed books I purchase?

Years ago, I asked myself the exact same question: how could it be that I'm reading a NYT bestseller and it's missing a period, or a 'the' or an 'a.' Chances are you have already found an error or two in this very book. Here's a fact: every printed book has an average of 6 errors. Imagine that! As I went through my first book with McGraw-Hill, I suddenly understood why.

- **Manual process is still a part of life**

Believe it or not, certain publishing houses still require the submission of a printed manuscript. The accepted version is edited, and returned to you, via Federal Express in my situations, marked up with red lines, queries and the like. I make my notes, and send it back. The next version I get has another set of markups, this time in another color. I make my comments and send it back. This occurs three to five times; all commentary in writing, in different colors. The last draft is so messy it resembles a Kandinsky painting.

- **Microsoft Word is imperfect**

Even before the above messiness happens, MS Word doesn't catch every grammatical and spelling error. When the final version is input into Word (or whatever program is used by your publisher), all sorts of new problems are introduced into your manuscript. Let's pretend that your original submitted manuscript was 100% error free. The comments, queries and changes from the aforementioned editors are now being incorporated. As a result, missing words, extra words, spaces and all kinds of grammatical typos are now in your "edited" manuscript.

- **Proofers are imperfect**

I recall my first visit to a publishing house. It was just before lunchtime, and as I walked by a cubicle, a woman was reading a book. On the way out, this same woman had her head down on her desk and she was sleeping. A cat nap, I was told. Made sense to me. It was lunch, she was tired, good for her, I thought, rather envious she possessed the ability to crash out at the office. The editor who accompanied me confided the role of the proofer was one of the hardest in the cycle.

"They aren't reading for pleasure but for errors," she said. "It gets monotonous." That's why the good publishing companies employ two proofers in the cycle; fresh eyes make for fewer errors. Even then, industry insiders acknowledge errors will still get through.

- **You are the final sign-off**

A blessing and a curse. By this time, you have endured multiple rounds of editing and two proof versions. You are so completely and utterly done that looking at your book yet again is about the last thing you want to do. Also, you are probably half-way through another manuscript that you are far more excited about. If you feel you can't do the final read justice, enlist a relative or neighbor. Trust me, everyone glories in finding typos.

A note on AP vs. Chicago Style guide: Once I hired a line editor who completed her task and handed off the manuscript to a copy editor. When I got it back, the manuscript was filled with red. I couldn't understand why and was very unhappy. So many inconsistencies. It took me a few discussions with both, until one said: "It appears I used the AP Style guide and she used the Chicago style guide." Arg! I had to pay both of course, because I hadn't specified which guide I wanted them to use. Lesson learned. When you are interviewing editors, especially line and copy, ensure they are using the same style guide.

By now, you are likely a bit overwhelmed with the information I've shared and depressed about the cost. You need to look at it this way: all in, your first book is going to cost you a nice, Mexican vacation for a family of four.

Yet at the end, you will have more than a nice tan and some souvenirs. You will have a book that is good enough to be sold on the open market or put into the hands of an agent or sent to a publisher who will have to do little or no work on it.

Still, you may not be convinced, because you are probably already working through the mechanics of hiring your neighbor, friends or relatives to do some of the line editing and proof reading for you at a lower cost than the amounts I mentioned above. Before you despair and stop writing altogether, I'm going to share another story of personal failure with you, one that converted me to hiring an editor, because I wasn't always a proponent of strategic editing, especially when I moved away from mainstream publishing and had to pay for it myself.

Recall my earlier story of being fortunate enough to get Peter Rubie as my agent, and how he eventually had to let me go because he couldn't sell my work. I then had a choice to buckle down and improve my writing or forever be consigned to being a writer of non-fiction.

What I didn't tell you was that it took me four years, count them, four years of obstinacy on my part, and frugality on the part of my husband, before I could take the next step and move forward with my goal to write fiction. The initial problem was with me—I didn't know what I didn't know, just like the reporter who had written his suspense book or the woman who wrote her fantasy novel. Because I couldn't articulate my deficiency to my husband in a way that would justify the initial expense, nor could I guarantee the eventual product would sell any better, I did nothing.

During those four years, I continued to write but I continued to write crap. Books that my agent wouldn't accept and I wasn't confident enough to try and sell on the open market. Four years of lost opportunity where I could have learned, improved and turned out meaningful works.

It wasn't one thing that pushed me over the edge. Instead I just woke up one day wanting to be honest about my skills. I had peaked as an author and wasn't going to get any better without help from a professional editor. That morning, I spoke with Roger and we had what I refer to as my "come-to-Jesus" moment. He agreed that we were either going to commit the money to my 'graduate school,' or I had to be content with writing books only I would read.

As you saw from the table 9, it took a while, especially for the women's contemporary fiction. But since then, the time to market has shrunk significantly. My writing has improved, as has the process of getting the book into the hands of readers. Do I wish I would have made the investment years earlier? Certainly, and I pass that counsel to you: don't wait. You likely require an editor if any one of the following things are happening in your authoring world:

1. **You aren't making any sales.**

If you are self-published and the books aren't moving, something's up. You can assign this to minimal or non-existent marketing, which may be the case. However, using the data point of 1200 book sales, if you have less than fifty, consider the reality it may be the quality of the content.

2. **You can't get an agent to look at your book or respond to your query.**

Agents are always looking for the next-bestselling author and want to read a new manuscript that captivates from page one. Most agents I know will read the first twenty pages. If they're not willing to do that with your manuscript, there's a problem.

Question 57: I don't know anyone in the industry. Where do I start?

You have two routes to find the right editor.

➢ **On-line forum: admin contact**. If you need a strategic editor and don't know a soul in the industry (e.g. agents, publishers etc.) you can look on-line on forums for editors and post a query to the administrator. Often, the admin will post your request because it's likely to result in a contract for someone in the forum.

➢ **On-line forum: direct post.** Forums for line or copy editors are often combined. When I was looking for a proof reader I found editors in the line and copy category were open to proof reading for a standard amount.

Question 58: What's the total cost of getting my book to market, including pre-marketing and sales?

As you know by now, it ranges, depending on the publishing route you take to market, the service providers you elect to use and the costs associated with each. Not all books require each role, and some editors can combine their efforts. In other words, look at this as the worst case (or in my first few books, a realistic case) scenario.

Table 11. Total cost of editing a 300-page book

Editor	Cost per hour	Total
Strategic editor	$95-$125/hour (2 rounds)	$2-4,000.00
Line editor	$45-$95/hour ($65x10)	$650.00
Copy editor	$45-$95/hour ($50x10)	$500.00
Proof reader 1	$15-$25/hour($20x8)	$160.00
Proof reader 2	$15-$25/hour ($20x8)	$160.00
		$3,770-5,770.00

Process, Tools and Time Management

CHAPTER HIGHLIGHTS

- *Start to finish*
- *Tools and process*
- *How the pros do it*

Writing has laws of perspective, of light and shade just as painting does, or music. If you are born knowing them, fine. If not, learn them. Then rearrange the rules to suit yourself.

Truman Capote

One of my favorite subjects is the writing process. It's because over the years, I've tried every technique recommended at workshops and conferences, as well as what I read in the best how-to's. None of them worked for me, so when I came across a process that did work, I felt like Moses in the desert when the manna started to fall from heaven. My favorite process is one I learned from the movie industry: blocking out the entire story into Acts. As I applied this to writing novels, it has become a no-fail, start-to-finish template I describe to anyone who will listen. As Truman Capote said, "Rearrange the rules to suit yourself." Once I found a writing process that worked, I began honing the details to fit my genre.

Question 59: What is the best writing process to follow? It seems like every author, teacher, workshop and book I buy tells me to do something different.

The best process to use is the one that works for you and you alone.

Focusing first on non-fiction, look at it like a term-paper, as I did. Writing non-fiction is adhering to an outline you have created. In my case, each chapter had five sub-sections, and each section had a specific idea to convey.

Fiction is a totally different scenario, and it took me a while to figure out what worked and what didn't. What follows is my process from start to finish that has now worked for my last five fiction books.

- **Step one: write the story outline**. I use a method I learned from the movie world. It's fast, effective and makes you clarify your thoughts. If you haven't done this before, or if an outline seems overwhelming, do what the movie people do (and I've adopted). **Create 3 acts**. Delineate your entire plot into a series of bullet points that are separated by three acts. Do NOT go into massive detail. Each act should be perhaps 20-25 bullet points. Also, purchase a small, spiral bound notebook that has tabs. I purchased mine for about $8 bucks at the local office supply store. I use less than a single tab for an entire book. This first exercise should take no more than 2 pages.

- **Step two: chapter by chapter, paragraph form.** This follows the bullet points you created in the first exercise. My chapter write out includes no more than 3-5 paragraphs for each chapter. The point of this is NOT to write the book, but to identify the major plot lines, character development, necessary transitions and basic scenes. The most valuable part of this process is to help you identify the ebbs and flows, the holes, weak or slow points in the book.

- **Step three: review and refine the story outline** Once you've done this work, put it down for a day or two, then come back to it and analyze each component. Specifically, you should review the outline for a) the major scenes and b) the major and minor characters. Are they showing up regularly? Did you remember to put in a secondary character to continue the sub-plot? Are you setting the scenes in Act 2 for closure in Act 3? Going through this exercise is invaluable. It saves hours of wasted effort on your part during your writing cycles and hundreds of dollars of editing and rewrite efforts.

> A book can be separated into 3 Acts. A good rule of thumb is each Act should have 2-3 major scenes. Write summary chapters inclusive of 3-5 paragraphs. Begin writing to that outline.

Question 60: What's after the outline?

- **Write your first draft adhering to the paragraph outline.**

You will find that a three to five paragraph summary quickly evolves into an eight to ten-page chapter. Another good rule of thumb is any chapter over fifteen pages needs to be cut or refined in order to keep the reader's attention.

Question 61: What other processes exist to create a visual story flow?

If the process I described doesn't resonate with your personality or style, perhaps two other approaches might appeal more.

When I was invited by the movie studio to participate in a three-day working session for *Chambers*, I was introduced to the movie-way of visualizing the plot of a book. This was transformative for me, and I summarized the approach in Question 58. I'll now give you the visual process for the same exercise.

- **Visual book development process**

On a wall, and with lots of different colored sticky note pads, three sections are created, each one representing an Act. You have three parallel, vertical sections, delineated by Act 1, Act 2 and Act 3.

Colors are assigned to each of the major and minor characters, as well as the major events and plot turns. Quite quickly, a four-hundred-page book is visually mapped out, giving anyone in the room the overall idea of the plot and characters at a glance. It's also a way to identify where the pacing of the story drags, or if gaps exist in the storyline.

➢ **Character profiling approach**

In Peter Rubie's well received book *Elements of Storytelling*, he provides a three-page character profiling list. This touches on one way to keep the characters straight. Others use notepads with tabs for each of the characters, plot lines, and intricacies.

Question 62: Can't I just let it flow? I've read so much about writing this way and it's always talked about at conferences and writer's workshops.

As a teen, I also read how some authors just "let it flow." In addition to this bit of advice, two others stand out. 1. Write the end first because this makes it easier to write the rest of the book (if you know where you are going you can get there easier). 2. If a scene comes to you, stop everything you are doing 'get it down.'

I've tried all three: let it flow, write the ending and write the scene down. Honestly, none have worked for me and here's why it might save you time to avoid these strategies.

➢ **Accurate but empty**

I found that while I could visualize an ending, the emotional build-up and little details required for a dramatic, impactful finale were absent. It was like going to a 4-star restaurant without eating the food. Very unsatisfying. As a result, it took only a few tries at this to realize I was wasting my time. **I knew where I wanted to go, and it was better to write my way there than to try the short-cut.**

- **Disjointed scenes**

Another technique I'd read about, tried and stopped using was "scene writing." This means that you can visualize a scene so clearly that you take the time to write it down, telling yourself you will slot it in later in the right place.

While it accomplished its goal (getting the entire scene down in a single shot), I learned through experience that it took me much longer to rework the scenes preceding and following it when I finally figured out where it needed to go in the storyline. The tone of the scene, the characters, details, even setting were usually all wrong.

- **Messy writing**

If writing to the outline constrains you, then by all means, do what I did about thirteen years ago with my first fiction book. I just "let it flow," a process that I'd read about as an impressionable teen. You know what came out of letting if flow? A lot of disjointed ideas, themes and characters.

That said, letting it flow is great for one thing: Writer's Block, and I addressed this a bit earlier in the book. The best use of free-form writing is in short spurts, where you pick a random idea and write free form for a finite period, say ten minutes. **Writing free form for a short period of time clears the brain, forcing you to think about a subject from opposing angles**.

Question 63: What do I do with all the scenes that I've created

(in my mind or on paper)?

You embrace the word patience. You think about it, visualize it, write it down, but stay the course and write the book in logical sequence.

Pause. I know you are screaming at me right now, shaking your head, telling me that you will not wait, you will do what you want and it will turn out fine. I'm with you as you say those words and I truly, honestly feel your emotional angst because I felt it too, with every ounce of my being. I was not going to constrain my creativity by using a dull process and I was certainly *not* going to be told (or listen to advice) from a published author lecturing me on what was the best way to write, because how could he/she know what I'm going through and capable of?

Deep breath. I was there. I get it. I lived it—for years. I'm only offering up what I learned from my years of obstinance. Had I listened, even a little, I wouldn't have wasted days/weeks/months/years of effort. My destination would have been reached far faster and with more success if I had tried to employ these lessons much sooner.

Question 64: How much does formatting play into the purchase of a book by a publisher?

The format for submissions is a standard 12 point double spaced manuscript. You can use a template provided by Microsoft Word. That said, it's never mattered a bit in my experience, and this is at two levels.

The first level is with your strategic editor. Right out of the gate, the editor I had hired requested 1.5 space and 11-point font. It's because the review conducted on the computer doesn't require a full double space, as edits are made electronically, directly into the file. Further, the editor usually wants to see as much on the page as possible. Reducing the font and spacing helps the editing process.

The second level is with the publisher. The first book I submitted conformed to this formatting but all the others were 11 pt. and 1.5 spaced. I've never received a comment about this or request to change my manuscript formatting.

Question 65: Where does word count come into play?

Picture this: you completed your manuscript and are ready to tell your editor/agent/publisher/project manager the great news. You are rightly proud of the many pages you have written.

"What's the word count?" you are asked. To this, you are stymied. You know the page count by heart not the word count. You have to look it up.

Word counts are far more important than the page count for the very reason I describe in question 61. Each book will have custom formatting, fonts, graphics, tables or illustrations. The person on the end of the phone is quickly factoring the word count into the number of pages, based upon what has been discussed internally.

Also, the editor/agent etc., can immediately tell you if the word count is too high and needs to be trimmed in order for the book to make a profit. Now that you are acutely familiar with the role page count plays in the profit of a book, you should be prepared for the editor/publisher to tell you your 120,000-word count book needs to drop to 90,000, or that your 80,000-word count book needs to be 110,000 based upon your genre expectations.

Question 66: Do I need a degree in creative writing?

No. Writing a novel is the great equalizer. The lack of a degree didn't stop Barbara Delinsky (stay at home house wife), Jackie Collins (expelled from school at 15), Tom Clancy (insurance salesman), or Amanda Hocking (physical therapist). Shall I go on? You must have an idea, the interest, the determination and perseverance to keep going as you perfect the ability to write down what's in your head.

Question 67: Do I need a computer?

J.K. Rowling used a pen and paper, writing in different cafes, trains and the like, because she couldn't afford a computer. Jackie Collins used a yellow legal pad and a pen as well. Authoring is the great equalizer because there is no barrier to competition. **If you can write words on a piece of paper, you can write a book.** Does a computer help? Sure, but only if you can type.

A side-note to this is the actual "tools," other than a computer that I've found helpful to have at hand. I'm raising this only because I fell into the annoying trap of so many novice authors: I felt that I needed an upright stand to hold my pages, and recall purchasing four of various shapes and sizes.

My wonderful find? A $12.00 ceramic cookbook holder (in red, but it also comes in white and black) from Target. It has two edges on either side and is deep enough to hold a big cookbook or a thick manuscript. I can put my pages side by side, and if the manuscript is so big it starts to slide (in the middle), I use a clip, either the kind for potato chips or the big, metal clips you find at a business supply store. I came upon this wonderful tool three years ago and have been using it ever since.

Question 68: Should I take special classes to help improve my writing skills?

Lots of strong opinions on this one and it comes down to need, perspective, time and sometimes money. Of all the authors mentioned earlier in question 57, I'm not aware of one who has stated he/she took a writing class. That's not to say they haven't attended writing classes or that such classes aren't valuable.

I'll admit to being highly influenced by John Grisham who said he wrote, he didn't go to class or sit in workshops. To take that further, the "classroom," in my opinion, doesn't always require an instructor. Bestselling and award-winning author Brandlyn Collins started writing when she was in her thirties, a mother of three young children. She told me of spending five years going to movies, watching how stories unfolded and reading the works of every bestselling author in her genre she could find, then dissecting the various approaches. She says it took another five years of applying those principles and techniques to write her first three-book series. Right out of the gate, she got a book deal for all three books. She created her own classroom and it worked well in her situation.

Another aspect of attending a writing class is the intangible attitude of confidence that can be felt when surrounded by like-minded, hopeful individuals and an instructor who patiently breaks down the process.

Where can you start? Consider the following:

➢ **Convenience and location**

Are you in the middle of farmland, with only the Internet as your local teacher? If so, you aren't going to have much of a choice but to use on-line teaching resources. More and more web-based seminars and workshops are being provided for authors in remote locales. Many authors, including myself, have created and posted videos that touch on aspects of authoring.

➢ **Qualification and relevance**

Your hometown might have colleges with a curriculum that may or may not apply to what you need at this stage in your career. Rudimentary writing? Creative writing? Technical writing? Perhaps you're not even sure what's going to be the style that fits the best for you.

Check out the curriculum, attend a few classes, talk to the

professors and maybe even audit the class (you pay the money but don't get a grade). This may reveal new types and ways of writing you haven't considered. Taking a grade in the course might also be quite beneficial, as it would give you an objective assessment of where you stand as a writer, both technically and creatively.

If sitting in a class for weeks doesn't fit with your situation, then consider the usefulness of a writer's group. Many exist, usually organized by genres and sometimes the state and stage of the author (e.g. published or aspiring).

A writer's group typically means individuals who gather together on a regular basis to critique each other's works. The actual agenda and format is completely dependent on the bi-laws of that group. Some focus on reading and reviewing each other's work. Others invited guest speakers with a Q & A session following. Check into the genre, the typical format and what you can reasonably expect to get out of the forum. Of course, maybe you just want to socialize with others in your industry, and this motivation alone may be all you need for now.

Where does that leave you?

"Writers conferences are for people who want to talk about writing, and don't actually write," John Grisham famously said. While this didn't endear him to the writing community (and he didn't care, because he's always said he's about the readers, not the industry), I was relieved I wasn't the only one who felt this way.

Doing is different that listening and talking.

If you have the money, the interest, availability and time, then experiment with local or regional classes in your area, but don't sacrifice the actual writing for endlessly attending forums about the art of writing when you need to be perfecting the act of writing.

Question 69: Do I backup my computer? What's a foolproof method?

If I could make certain sections red, this would be one of them.

Back-up your data often and place the files on different drives. During the last round of work on *Chambers*, which had by this time been optioned for film and had two foreign publishing deals, my computer failed; melted down to the point where I couldn't get the files —a complete and total loss of all the data. I'd not backed-up my computer for two months—that's a lot of time in the life of an author. I'm paranoid and never backed up to the "cloud," be it Dropbox, Google or anything else.

Frantic, I searched for any and all hardcopies, but those were also two months old. Then Roger came to the rescue.

"What was the latest version you sent to Pam?" Pam Liflander served as the strategic editor on the project, and sure enough, she had my most recent copies. They were only two weeks old, which was still traumatically painful, because I had to rewrite and make all the changes I had just completed. The silver lining, however, was I was so pressed for time, my writing was sharper than it had been previously.

Backing up your work:

- **The cloud.** If you are comfortable, put your work up on a cloud (Internet) based storage application.
- **Hard storage device.** Once a month (or every two weeks depending) back-up your writing on a separate and distinct drive. I purchased a small, iPhone 5s sized brick that uses a USB plug. These are about $50 or less.
- **Emailing yourself.** After the *Chambers* experience I regularly email major revisions of my work to my alternate email accounts, those I can access from anywhere on any device. This is simply more convenient for me because I can then easily forward files to an editor, agent or publisher.

Question 70: Are there forums or events where I can connect with other authors in my genre?

Connecting with other authors is very different from sitting in a class or workshop to learn strategies and tactics. If this is your goal, then yes, there are many events you can attend, by city, state, region, genre and subject. A simple search by genre will yield all you need to know and more.

> If you like attending conferences for professional networking, skill development or pure motivation, you have plenty of options.

For example, if you are interested in romance, you should check out Romance Writers of America (rwa.org). It has a full conference list for 2018-2019 at all levels, national and regional. For a global/local view of conferences in the romance field, I prefer Romancerefined.com which has a section on events and forums.

In the suspense/mystery/thriller world, take a look at Sleuthfest, sponsored by the Florida Chapter of Mystery Writers of America. This year the keynote is David Baldacci, a big name. For independent or self-published authors, the Independent Author's Conference, held in Philadelphia this year and next, is one of many you can attend. It attracts publishers in the genre, sales and marketing professionals and quite a few published authors as well.

Whatever your genre or status, enter a query for your genre, review the speakers and topics and allocate some time and money for the event.

Question 71: What about attending a conference to meet a prospective agent or publisher?

Yes, conferences can be an excellent place to meet prospective agents and publishers if it is the right one for your genre. I know two aspiring authors who have established relationships with both an agent and publisher respectively at conferences, with the caveat that in both instances, the venues were held in New York.

Question 72: I feel like my story is strong but my writing hasn't caught up. Any advice?

"Creating a book is like making a cake, one part talent, one part recipe," said Peter one day. He went on to say that the talent is what you bring to the table that's unique: your idea, storyline, plot, etc. Originality is what's going to make you stand out from the crowd and capture and hold the attention of the reader. The recipe is the technical aspects of the book, and by this, I mean the structure of the sentence, the style of writing, the grammar and everything else that makes a reader stick with a book and not put it down.

Peter, who if you recall, took me on, dumped me, then took me on again when I improved, continued. "You have great ideas but weak execution."

"What is weak execution?" I asked him, bothered not in the least by the comment. As a businesswoman first (because that's what paid the bills for many years), and author second, I wasn't concerned with the criticism, I wanted solutions.

> Redundancy check: it's easy to unconsciously use a word more than once in the same paragraph or the same page. You may not notice but the reader will. Periodically check words to reduce redundancy.

"What am I doing wrong? What can I change?" I asked him. (I recall posting the question with a flat voice, but inside, I was plaintively, desperately whining). Peter essentially told me my story, character and plot were strong, but my writing—the execution, hadn't caught up. Here's what else he told me, and what I want to share with you.

➢ **Style**

Are you writing first person, third…what? In my first attempt at fiction, I'd used three points of views. "Ambitious," was how Peter had diplomatically described it. I was obtuse, so he had to be clearer.

"Three voices are hard for even the most skilled writer. Choose a single point of view long enough to master it." After multiple attempts to adapt the manuscript, I ultimately gave up. It was easier to start over with an entirely new idea than to change my vision to a completely new writing style.

➢ **Editing**

I've already devoted an entire chapter to the value of editing. Once I transitioned from thinking editing was someone else's job and embraced an editor's edits, my writing dramatically improved.

➢ **Writing**

"Have you heard the 10,000-hour rule?" Peter asked me one day when I was saying something along the lines of "how long is this going to take?" (Okay, that was more whine than asking). Confessing I'd not heard this particular rule, he enlightened me.

"It's the conventional wisdom for how long it takes a person to become expert in a skill. Opera singing, for example," he continued, referencing his wife who sang on Broadway for almost twenty years. "Or myself, with jazz." I figured that Peter, a man who plays multiple instruments and moonlights in a jazz group, knew what he was talking about. But it wasn't just the arts. Free throws are included too, he said, citing that and other technical skills that take 10,000 hours of practice to perfect.

"The key is not how long you practice but what you practice in order to get better," he continued. "The quickest way to learn how to play fast is to first, play super, super slowly, because you have concentrate really hard on what's in front of you. Then you can play fast easily."

I'm not sure what I mumbled in response as I calculated how long I'd spent at the craft of authoring up to that point. I hadn't even reached a thousand hours. I moaned. It was going to take me years to be a good writer. But by that evening, pragmatism had set in. The time was going to pass regardless, so I might as well do something with it. And yes, you've read that before. It's my go-to pump-me-up comment when I'm feeling I will never be as good, as successful and as content as I want to be.

Question 73: What if I'm halfway through my book and I hate it?

Then you set it aside (don't ever throw it away,) and give it a rest. You may come to realize parts of the book are salvageable but overall the plot went off track. If it can be resurrected, then pick it up again when you have figured out the problem areas. If you can pay an editor to read it, go in that direction. In the absence of a budget for such a read, then turn to a trusted source who will be honest.

If the project truly is dead to you, then take a break, clear your mind and start fresh—but don't throw it away. At some point in the future, you will take great satisfaction in pulling it out, dusting it off, and recognizing how far you've progressed. Who knows? You may even smile a bit and say 'that wasn't half bad.'

Question 74: What does a writing schedule look like?

One that is consistent and the most productive for your situation.

Back in Chapter Two, a question about 'finding the time' was addressed and I identified 20-minute blocks as being a good starting point. Are these actual writing minutes, on a computer? Not necessarily. "Writing" is an umbrella category for:

- development (you are writing down the ideas and outline)
- editing (revising what you have written)
- actual writing. Not all environments are conducive to writing; you may not feel safe taking a computer on the bus, but a notepad works just fine.

Now take a look your average day and consider when you have both the time and mental clarity to write, in whatever format that might take. Keep in mind that this will likely adjust from month to month or year to year, along with your own life changes.

- Morning schedule: prior to work or before your day gets going. You rise early, go straight to the computer and get in an hour.
- Afternoon schedule: you get on the train and write, or return home from work and dedicate an hour before or after the gym or before your kids get home.

- You set aside hours on the weekend: a block of 2-4 hours/day.

Question 75: How to I start building a writing schedule?

Start by paying attention to your schedule and tally where you are spending your time.

If you have ever been on a diet, the first task is to track your food. It's a way to understand your triggers and habits as it relates to what you consume. The approach to writing is no different, and at some point, you need to view it as an effort, just like a dietary program you are following.

As you track and allocate your available time, you will be faced with a lot of temptations, like a person on a diet who is asked to attend a Thanksgiving dinner. Over and over, you will need to make a choice, so know your answer in advance in order to eliminate temptation.

Ask and answer these questions well before you get into the situation.

- What is the value of those activities that occupy your time?
- Are you building relationships (e.g. with your kids, family or significant other)?
- Is the activity worth sacrificing your personal dream for temporary pleasure/fun/distraction?

All that adds up to hours every week that you can be using to realize your dream.

I write/edit in the morning when my brain works better. Then I tackle business tasks in the afternoon. I don't time manage. I make a weekly list of things I need to do and use that list as my push to complete everything.

Eliza Green

Question 76: What advice to you have to stick to a schedule?

To be a good author, you need to be as strict with your schedule as you are with other life priorities.

As you are wondering where in the world you are going to find the time to write in an already packed day, think of Rachel, the aspiring author with multiple health issues. Aspiring novelist Rachel Parker committed to the twenty-minute a day rule in July 2017. At that point, she had roughly seventy pages completed. Given her physical limitations, she knew that her best times were the morning and early evening. She changed her schedule to fit with her particular needs, and has stuck to her writing, morning and early evening, for five months. The output was dramatic.

"I am now one chapter out, and think a few sections need small re-writes." The novel is about 350 pages. Her secret is commitment.

"No matter where I am or what I'm doing, I keep to my writing schedule. On vacation, visiting family, it doesn't matter." Nothing gets in her way or keeps her from her goal.

Here are a few of my own personal habits (although you may call them strange quirks).

I limit my lunch events/meetings or social activities to no more than one a week. I've not watched television in nearly fifteen years. And professional sports? I've attended one MLB game and zero, nada, nothing any other sport.

Do I feel like I've had to give up everything in order to write? No. I simply have higher priorities. **I don't want to watch someone else living their dream, I want to create my own dream**. That doesn't happen without sacrifice. It's now worth it, once again pointing to the twenty-year overnight success. What started as a hobby has evolved to a career, but that career started long before it was my full-time occupation.

How strict is my schedule? Strict. I'm strict about what I don't do, but I also maximize every moment I can.

- **My "off-time."** On the plane I have my computer in my bag and whip it out once the kids are settled. Roger, my husband reads, sleeps or watches movies. I write.
- **In the car**, on a long trip, after we have talked for hours, Roger knows I'm antsy to write. He zones out to music and I take out my computer.
- **My wait time**. Waiting for the doctor appointment to begin, the tires are being rotated, and the singular lunch appointment/event who is late. I take out my notebook or computer and do what? Write.

Question 77: I've read so much about being in "the zone" with the perfect environment. Is it a physical state or mental?

Like nearly all other authoring subjects, this one is open to debate. Nate Kreuter, a professor of writing, wrote a piece on the subject[2] describing what he tells his first and second year college students.

Kreuter contends two environments exist: the physical and the social, one being your actual external environment and the other is your mental state. When the two states are in sync, it's that comfortable place where creativity meets productivity. The downside is that patterns lead to complacency, then a dullness of mind, eventually stifling creativity. Kreuter himself tries to match the type of activity or writing with the environment. Initial drafting is at a busy coffee shop, but actual writing, happens at home where he has no distractions.

Kreuter's findings would have been good for me to know about twenty years ago, but I'm not sure I would have taken his words on faith. I probably would have done exactly what I did: figured out what environment works best for me.

---

[2] Nate Kreuter, Inside Higher Ed, May 19, 2014, Writing Environments

> *There is no ideal writing environment. The ideal is the set of circumstances that allows you to be productive.*
> *Nate Krueger, writing professor*

Non-fiction research and writing: my home office, which is actually my dining room table. A quirk of mine is I have a guest home that I'd originally thought would be my writing mecca, just like John Grisham. He would go upstairs, lock the door and write.

Not me. I'm exactly what Kreuter describes: I have a social aspect as well as an environment need that I require. I want my kitchen close, my dog closer, and the freedom to pipe in music if I so choose. So, the dining room table it is. I look out over the valley and onto the lake and I'm in my happy zone.

Fiction research: mostly at the library.

Fiction writing: never, *ever* at the table or in any kind of antiseptic environment. It's on my couch, in my comfortable chair, on the deck, or anywhere else I feel transported.

Question 78: Can you give me ideas for my own writing life so I can replicate it?

Sure, but first, let me set the stage.

Writing began when I had no kids, the opportunity for lots of travel and extra time at my disposal. I completed my first two books. When I became pregnant, I was put on bedrest and had huge blocks of time, with literally nothing to do but watch television or write (and you know how I feel about watching TV). I gave birth to two more books, just like my two children, one after another.

Then a writing lag occurred. The only time I wasn't tired and without distractions was during naptimes; that's when I write. This lasted for not quite two years, when naps ended and so practically, did my writing. First it stalled, then ended entirely, hence, the twenty minutes adage. It was one of the most frustrating periods of my life, because I had to take a four-year life pause. My schedule finally got back on track when my youngest started pre-school and has increased every year. **Very few authors have the luxury of eight-hour blocks of uninterrupted writing, which I still don't have.**

When I write:

- **My wait time** (after dropping kids off and my yoga class.)
  - 4 days per week, in the car. **50 min/day= @3.5 hours**
- **My home time**. 3 hours before I turn around and get the kids.
  - 3 days a week at my house, **2 hrs= 6 hours**.
- **At night**. After the kids are in bed.
  - 2-3 nights/wk, 1 hr **=3 hrs**
- **On the weekend**, if I'm lucky= **6 hrs**
- **Once a week**, maybe, I'll have a good stretch of four to six hours
  - **5 hrs.**

That puts me at about **24 hours a week**. Is it a bit disjointed? Yep.

Have I learned to be flexible? Sure. But it's proof that if you focus your time, energy and effort you can make time for writing.

As Kreuter noted, one thing is guaranteed: over time, your writing habits and schedules will change. Go with it. Also recognize that the more successful you become, the more time you will spend on the business aspect of authoring. The percentage of time spent writing will drift from 80-90 percent writing and 10-20 business, then to 60-40, until it may even swing the other direction, where business takes over the majority of your schedule.

Conducting Interviews and Fact Checking

CHAPTER HIGHLIGHTS

- *Interviewees & liable*
- *Fact checking*
- *How the pros do it*

The world is full of people with information-compulsion who want to tell you their stories. They want to tell you things that you don't know. They're some of the greatest allies that any writer has.

Tom Wolfe

You would think that most people would be flattered to be included in a book that will be read by hundreds or thousands of people, but often they aren't. Including *Author Straight Talk*, I've written five non-fiction books where I have interviewed other people. Out of the approximately 125 people interviewed, (@ 25 per book), very few were initially interested. And do you know why? It wasn't the subject matter, but me, the author.

You read that right. The author. Without a brand name magazine behind me (that I suppose could be sued) or a list of published books, the first interviewees had to be convinced to participate. My response was to create a pitch letter that I'll explain in this chapter, along with associated documents and my personal commitment to the interview subject.

The second part of interviewing and writing is fact-checking. The author's role has changed over time, the burden of this job moving from the publisher largely to the author. After stumbling the first time out, I had the chance to learn from the best, and have followed a professional-level protocol ever since. No author wants to be sued. Between interviewing and fact-checking you can prevent this unfortunate but increasingly common circumstance.

Question 79: How do I prevent getting sued by a subject I'm writing about?

Authors and journalists must adhere to a different set of standards for public figures than a private individual. A public figure—celebrity, politician, even a fellow author, have fewer rights than does a private citizen. The Journalism Code of Ethics followed in the US is worth reading, but to summarize, if an author only has a single source for a reference, the author must cite the reference. However, if two or more individuals are on record as citing the same fact, commentary, etc., sourcing is not required.

Saving the author

The essential concern and risk for the author is that a reference, comment, allegation or conclusion will financially harm someone. It is this harm to reputation or financial earning capability that becomes the essence for a lawsuit. As such, data provided by more than one source transitions the context from a single-source to a multi-source situation, further insulating the author.

I'll give you an example of how this protected me, the author, when I wrote the authorized biography of Sue Kim.

During the research phase, I interviewed over seventy-five people who had different levels of contact with Sue, relatives and friends, peers and acquaintances who had worked with her for decades. I was told that certain individuals were liars, thieves, ex-cons, domestic abusers, chronic gamblers, alcoholics and more. These "recollections" become accusations when put on to paper.

Knowing that I'd be facing scrutiny years down the road, I followed a two-step approach. At the beginning of the interview I asked and received permission to record the interview.

Then I received a verbal acknowledgement (on tape) that anything that was said could be used in the book. While the interview was recorded, I also took notes. Each and every statement, opinion and assertion were cited when it was from a single individual, but when I had two or more persons making the same comment about an individual, then I didn't source it in the book. Even so, I have kept records of all the individuals and commentary for my own files, just in case.

The book was published over a year ago, but it's only been recently that I've been contacted by the families of individuals quoted who have since passed away, and others who are living, who disagree with the representations of their life and contribution to Sue's history. Additionally, I've had other individuals claiming responsibility and credit for key elements of her success. Had I not gone to the extent of recording and cataloging the interviews, I could be on the receiving end of challenging discussions at best and lawsuits at worst. As it was, my conversations weren't necessarily pleasant, but the individuals on record had made the statements. All I had done was write it down, source it and get the book published.

Question 80: When I take inspiration from a real person or experience, how do I ensure they won't come after me?

According to the code of ethics for journalism and authors, an author is free to write about a real person, either by using their name or making them anonymous. This holds true for both public figures or private individuals, some who have undergone horrible events such as the murder of a child. **The key for the author is to ensure that the writing isn't libelous, in other words, what's written is fact and doesn't materially damage the individual being written about.**

Going back to the Sue Kim project, I could still be liable for a lawsuit by the heirs/relatives of those I interviewed if I didn't cite the sources. According to the US journalism ethics standards, if a comment or statement has only one source, it must be attributed to a named individual. If, however, that fact is sourced by two or more individuals, those sources don't need to be identified. In my book, I was sure that all my sources were named, and I went so far as to gather, photocopy and catalogue those sources, along with written notes and tapes of the interviews. Even then, I've had several sources come back and dispute what they said on the record and in writing.

More information on the **subject of libel** can be found by running a search for Journalism Code of Ethics, which pulls up the Society of Professional Journalists. The section on creative writing and narrative non-fiction describes the standards an author must meet in order to be protected against a lawsuit.

Question 81: What if I'm writing about someone and it's flattering?

Even when you think you've created a completely flattering, bullet-proof likeness in your book, the original subject may not be happy. I learned this lesson as well. In *A Convenient Date*, I modeled an attorney on a former corporate lawyer who I greatly admire. When I told him he was the inspiration for the character in my book, he turned serious and asked that I not mention his name or his firm. He also asked I not tell anyone he was my inspiration. Initially, I thought it was funny, but then worried he had a deeper concern he wasn't revealing to me. "What's the real problem?" I asked.

"Please don't be offended," he said in his British accent. "But I don't want to be associated with a women's fiction novel."

I retorted he should be grateful I didn't kill him off. He laughed and once again repeated his request that he didn't want to be identified in any way whatsoever. I sent him a printed copy of the book, which he later admitted he never read. He said that he trusted me enough that he didn't need to read the book to ensure I'd honored his request, but I suspect the real reason he never read the book was because he wasn't going to deign to read a women's fiction novel.

No matter how good you make a person look, they will never be satisfied. It's better to use an individual for inspiration and keep your mouth shut as to their real identity. It's your own secret.

Question 82: When writing about celebrities, people or brands, do I have to get permission?

Nope, because public figures are just that—public. Did you know that neither movies made about Steve Jobs or the one on Jeff Zuckerberg (The Network) required permission from the family or estate? Someone—anyone—can write a book or produce a movie about me, or you, without our permission, even though you may not be a public figure. The key to the finished work is that it's not detrimental to the subject's reputation, and therefore not harmful.

Question 83: An individual is accusing me of writing about him/her, and I've totally invented the character. What do I do?

Unless you are going to totally offend the person, you laugh and say that next time you will try and be more original. Seriously, this happens a lot, and you will certainly learn quite a bit about the person making the comment. I have two people in my life who, after reading nearly every novel I've write, will inquire as to why (said character) is mirrored after them. I refer to my mother and my husband.

It's become a joke, but it highlights another downfall of being an author. Any and all individuals in your network may project themselves into or onto a character in your novel. More than once I've found myself completely caught off guard when a person has accused me directly or subtly of doing this, but I laugh it off. Generally, I say something like: "I had no idea you were into that or I would have asked you for more details." Whatever quip works the best for the situation, use it.

Question 84: How do I approach and convince the reluctant interviewee to speak with me?

You are upfront about the purpose of the project, identify the other interviewees who have agreed to participate, describe the general scope of the questions, and explain your commitment to fact-check/double check their quotes before you go to print. This may seem like overkill, but it's not. In today's society, interview subjects are wary of being set-up, duped and wrongly portrayed, either in print of broadcast. As paranoia grows, so should the caution exercised by the author.

Think of Megan Kelley, who interviewed the controversial Alex Jones for her news show while she was at Fox. He was dubious as to her intentions and recorded their initial conversation, wherein Kelley promised she wasn't going to set him up. During the actual interview, she went after him, just as he suspected. He then released the tape that was verified as authentic, showing Kelley hadn't acted with the level of integrity many thought was required by a journalist. Was she going to go to jail or be sued over it? No, but she took a serious hit to her reputation as being fair and honest.

The incident serves as a cautionary tale for the author who approaches a subject. The interviewee is as smart as you are. Be honest, be upfront and be consistent and you won't run into trouble.

Question 85: Do I cold-call an interview subject or provide a document for the potential interviewee to review?

You can do both, but ideally you have a personal introduction or reference. If not and you must contend with a gatekeeper, such as an assistant, then it's good to have a template document that can be sent ahead for review and vetting. Early on, I ran into this with nearly every interviewee subject, so to ease the process, I created a document which clearly articulates the primary points of my project. (I make this available on my website for you to use). If you are creating one yourself, be sure to include the following:

- **The Context**

The 'what, why and how' of the book and what I call the project overview. This is extracted directly from either my publisher pitch, the preface or the back of the book cover, depending on the stage of my writing.

- **The Relationship**

Identifying the terms between the author and the interviewee. Items such as compensation (none), copyright ownership, release and the like are clearly articulated.

- **Participants**

It's a truth that people want to be in good company. Give a high-level description of the other individuals who are contributing to your work. Name names if you can. Chances are high that one interviewee will recommend another for the book once the interview has been completed and you've done a good job.

- **Structure of the interview**

In-person, on the phone or via email, I've used a blend of all three for four books and have found one consistency: I get lower quality, usable material in-person. For whatever reason, the individual can be distracted (phone, interruptions) and the conversation tends to veer off track into conversational topics. This is fine if you have the time and are developing a long-term relationship with the individual, but not if you have a very specific set of answers that need to be culled.

- **Review/fact-checking**

My interviewee template identifies that I will validate any quotes provided for review and approval prior to publication. It is a key factor in gaining the reluctant interviewee's agreement of participation. More on this topic in the following section.

For a template you can use, I'm going to be adding The Interview Worksheet to my website so you can use it for free. I've used it for three non-fiction books. Using it yourself should save you some time.

Question 86: What is my role in fact checking?

In the "good old days," publishers employed an in-house fact-checker who would take the manuscript and contact each one of the subjects referenced in the book. Much of the processes and methodologies used in publishing was already underway in 2000 due to shrinking and sourcing more of the work. The timing was coincidental with 9/11 but the impact was immediate: more consolidation and personnel cuts.

Not long after the terrorist attacks occurred, I was notified I would be responsible for fact-checking my own book. My book had completed final edits and mentally, I was already out on the road, promoting my book at speaking events, smiling broadly as I signed copies that still had that new book smell. To be told I had to pause all my efforts and contact each and every one of the subjects was beyond frustrating.

Yet, I did it. Two weeks later, I'd reached all two dozen individuals, going through each word and sentence. But in my zeal to get the quotes right, I didn't check the spelling of the last name of the one of the subjects—a man who also happened to be a billionaire and the CEO of a publicly traded company. He was also a former client.

"How can that be?" you are asking yourself, appalled and perhaps even placing a hand over your mouth at the same time. (Recall that this was years before the Sue Kim project and I hadn't quite gotten the system down).

The bottom line is it slipped through, the book was published and I sent copies to everyone who had graciously contributed to the book. After receiving the signed copies at his office, his assistant called to inform me it had arrived and told me of the error. It was the pure definition of mortification, and I am reminded of my impatience every time I look at the book on my shelf.

Your role

In today's publishing world, most of the fact-checking responsibility has fallen to the author. And to clarify, offering the interviewee the entire manuscript to read or review is very different from fact-checking, reviewing or editing the quote.

- An author who has interviewed a subject for a book should read or provide the quote to the interview prior to the final version.

- The subject confirms the quote is accurate.
- The most respected publications go a step further and provide the preceding sentence (or paragraph), then the quote and the following sentence/paragraph. When placed in this context, the author's work/perspective is not being changed nor is the subject editing out the material, but the 'fact" or statement is validated.

Now I can just hear you thinking to yourself, "Times have changed and nowadays, I don't have to share the final work with my subjects." I get this perspective. Doing this fact-checking takes a lot of time at several stages during the project. First, during the actual writing and then during the editing process, but it's worth it because you have established a trust-based relationship with your subjects from the outset. To withhold the opportunity for accuracy from the subject will only ensure they don't support your book (either by word of mouth to friends or the community at large) when it appears. The other approach to take is the long-view, the one wherein you will be sending this individual your book and hoping he or she purchases copies for friends, employees and/or customers. This person may also be a referral source for future books. The bottom line is that every interviewee should be viewed as a lifelong contact you should value. Valuing that relationship starts by respecting the person enough to get the quotes validated.

Question 87: How do the "Pros" fact check?

Not long after the incident with the misspelled name, I was fortunate enough to see how a "real organization" fact-checked their material.

David Kirkpatrick, then a senior editor at *Fortune Magazine*, had read about my partner development business in a local San Francisco publication. He called me out of the blue and told me he wanted to write an article about me and my firm. While most young entrepreneurs would have jumped for joy, I tried to convince him otherwise. My company was young and I didn't want any competition.

I was a reluctant interviewee.

He skipped right over the part of trying to cajole me into participating. He essentially told said he was going to write the article with or without my involvement because he thought it was an interesting story. Faced with the choice of being unable to keep my company under wraps or getting the national attention of a premier magazine without having any input, I went from being a reluctant interviewee to a participant.

During this process, I observed how Kirkpatrick interviewed clients, employees and peers, and heard reports of his non-biased approach. A few weeks later, I received a call from a fact-checker at *Fortune*. It was through that experience that I learned how Kirkpatrick interpolated what I'd told him and while some of the words were different, the concept and more importantly, the intent was accurate. Being on the "other side" of the coin, the fearful, I'm-going-to-be-misquoted side was an invaluable way to learn the importance of the trust-based connection between the author and the subject.

The *Fortune* fact-checking team sent me an email with the paragraphs that included my quote, as well as preceding and following paragraphs. I was told that *Fortune*'s way of double checking was to get a written confirmation of content. That way, the final product is indisputable.

Learning from that experience, I built my own interviewee document. I've learned that while some subjects are fine fact-checking over the phone, others do want a written copy.

You can stipulate your process in the interviewee document. Subjects will vary in their desire for email or hard copy. Executives of a certain type (the really wealthy or busy) want email. Those who are retired or are old school, want hard copies. I'm flexible and do what makes it easiest for the subject because I learned my lesson: accuracy over speed and patience isn't a virtue. It's a necessity to save your reputation.

The Fact Checking Steps

- Before the interview, provide a summary of the project
- Attain a verbal confirmation recording the interview is OK
- Upon writing your piece, call and read the quote, perhaps providing the paragraph before and after for context
- Send a written note (email) of the quote and receive confirmation and approval
- Send a copy of the finished product

Marketing and Publicity

CHAPTER HIGHLIGHTS

- *Marketing scorecard*
- *Positioning and social media*
- *Genres and publishing norms*

Writing a book without promoting it is like waving to someone in a dark room. You know what you have done but nobody else does.

Madi Preda

As Peter said to me one day, "There is a big difference between marketing a book and making sales." So true, but it wasn't evident to me until I moved from non-fiction to fiction.

This chapter isn't intended to be the end-all thesis on how to market your book. Plenty of others are devoted to the subject. I know, because I have literally spent hundreds of dollars to find the secret sauce of the best book on marketing. You know what I found? Peter was right, again. Marketing a book, or yourself as an author, doesn't necessarily translate to book sales.

I'm going to highlight what has worked and what hasn't, keeping one primary message in mind: **marketing is creating awareness and demand for a product or servic**e, in this case, you, the author and your book.

Sales, on the other hand, is the conversion of that branding into the purchase of the product—your book. I've separated that subject into the following chapter, because it includes very tactical programs to start, increase and maintain sales.

Question 88: Why separate out marketing and sales? Aren't they connected?

Yes, they are connected but most of the world hasn't attended business school, and so generally confuse the two terms.

Think of it this way: when you create awareness for yourself (the author) and your books (the product) you are establishing a position in the minds of the reader: who you are, what you represent, the genre in which you write, the author promise you are making to the reader and so on. This is called positioning. **It is vital to correctly position yourself when you start out, and becomes even more important as your library of books grows.** The marketer's nirvana is that you, John Smith or Abby Grant, have successfully carved out a niche in the marketplace.

Once you have established your position with the target audience (let's say the 18-25 romance market) then you must instill a sense of urgency or desire to actually purchase the product. Just because I like Cindy Crawford's hair and makeup choices doesn't mean I'm going to buy her skincare line or her towels. A reader must be compelled to purchase. The activities that incentivize that purchase are called sales programs. Such things include discounts, giveaways and of course, the word itself—sale. It's the number one tool retailers and manufactures use to get the consumer to stop dithering and buy.

Question 89: Is marketing a book different from marketing other products?

When it comes to non-fiction, the answer is no. From the early reviews to the sales, the processes to market and position a book are nearly identical as many other products. It's the marketing of fiction where the world turns-upside down and all the rules are broken. Let me provide some context.

During fifteen years working in marketing and business development, I'd brought multiple products to market. This mean getting early adopters on board (analysts), customers (readers), product placements (book reviews), then blitzing a clearly identified target market with a critical mass of advertising and publications to get the word out. **I relied upon a long-held and proven statistic that a customer won't purchase a new product without at least twelve touching points, either visual (television, billboard, flyer**

etc.) or verbal (radio).

When it came to launching my first book, which was non-fiction, that process worked perfectly. The early reviews, pre-launch events, radio and television publicity and interviews, all helped to support a groundswell of momentum of coverage. The book made it on to a number of bestseller lists, including the Harvard business books for that year. The second time around, with *The Overlooked Expert* (first edition), I used the process again, and the sales of this book outsold my debut almost seven to one. While some of this might well have been due to the subject matter, I suspected a large part was my proficiency in marketing.

> I applied the same marketing approach to my fiction books that had proved so successful with my non-fiction. To my shock (and agent, movie studio etc.), it completely failed.

Then came fiction

When I applied these same principles to my fiction books, the initial aspect of the marketing was actually easier. The press was eager to write an article about a new book and author in the local area. Thanks to a few events I created that involved youth ages 12-18 in the community, the local television stations showed up. In fact, from a pure marketing perspective, the immediate results outweighed my previous book launches: more articles (five, front-page profiles in a five-city area around Seattle), three local television stations covering the event along and two of the best known on-line blogs wrote pieces.

Then came the results. We had less than fifty—count them, fifty, pre-orders of the book. Hundreds of thousands of impressions and very few pull-throughs:

The lessons learned were many, but I'm giving you the top-line.

- Press doesn't translate to sales, but it embedded me in the minds of the local media, readers, and bookstore owners.
- The local bookstore owners were impressed by the coverage, but they wanted to know why the sales weren't pulling through.
- The editors/reporters/tv hosts were interested in covering me, the author, an early-forties, formerly successful business person turned fiction author. That made an interesting story, but the book was secondary.
- The book itself, written for the older YA market of 14-18, weren't reading papers, watching morning television shows, or standing in line when we did a give-away with a bigshot movie producer from Los Angeles. The majority of people who showed up were men, over the age of 25. Both the producer and I were surprised, but he was pleasantly so. That male demographic is a huge target market for action-adventure movies (they go repeatedly to the theatre, spend money on every variation of the digital form and are loyal). I, the author, was clueless and just digested the information.

Question 90: Do traditional marketing programs have a value? And what does the effort look like?

Traditional marketing is considered public relations and advertising. And yes, it does have a value: to effectively brand yourself as an author. For my first four books, I used every traditional marketing tool available to me. After that, I didn't need or want another profile piece on me as a human being or author. I wanted sales.

Still, traditional marketing can and does have a value. The following table lists the essentials for a traditional marketing campaign.

Table 13. Traditional media and marketing activities

Activity	When used	Coverage	Result
Local press -tv, papers -blogs	Within 1 wk of the launch	City, region	Branding, invitations to other events
Local events -retail stores (not bookstores)	On or around book launch up to 45 days post	City, region	Branding, invites to speak at other events
Bookstore events	Day of launch or within 10 days	City, region	Branding, sales
Library readings	30 days before and after launch	City	Invites to speak at other events
School events -college or appropriate venue	Usually after launch	City, region	Branding, credibility
Book-themed events	Around the time of launch	City, region	Branding, press coverage

Most of these are self-explanatory and are well-covered in other books, including my own. How to contact an organization, what to say in your pitch (or verbal proposal), as well as scheduling and timing the events are detailed in several chapters of *The Overlooked Expert*, the 10th Anniversary Edition. The goal isn't to get you to purchase another book. Rather, it's to save this space for what I'd advise my earlier self to do if I had a second chance.

➢ **Focus on one or two events** that can be covered by the press, be it TV, print or blog. The visual communicates more than a static write-up. If you don't have a launch party at a bookstore, concoct a unique event that draws the media in.

For *Chambers*, I held a volcano making contest at the Seattle Science Center, invited the premier volcanologist from the University of Washington, and promoted the event to all the schools in the region. The professor and the science center donated the space and time. The professor brought an associate who judged the competition. I showed up with copies of my book (which sold) and the awards. Local television stations and the major newspaper covered the event. Besides all that, over sixty kids entered and the afternoon was a blast, with all sorts of volcanos blowing up. All this for a time travel adventure novel that features volcanos.

➢ If your book is non-fiction trade (business), contact the **local business groups** and pitch yourself as a speaker on the topic. It will likely be an unpaid appearance (more on this in Chapter Nine), and unlikely to be attended by a reporter, but it will be listed in local event sections in the paper and on-line.

➢ Do the same with **schools**, where appropriate. You won't be able to sell your book, but you are building a resume as a contributor of content.

➢ **Bookstore events.** Local bookstores love to support independent authors. The biggest hurdle faced is a poorly edited book or a dull personality that doesn't excite the bookstore owner/manager. Create a unique angle, pitch an off-time of the month that you know isn't already taken on the bookstore's calendar. Do keep in mind that some bookstores, particularly the chains, have rules in place such as a visiting author must be published by a mainstream house, not self-published.

> Allocate a portion of your time for local events. Getting in front of the right people can lead to a lot of revenue down the road.

These various marketing efforts did one thing very well: they branded and positioned me in the local and regional press.

If you look at the results column, quite a few of those include invitations to speak elsewhere. That's where the real money is, and I detail Author Options in Chapter Nine. Effective branding and positioning do one thing for an author: it places a value on your time and knowledge, which companies and entities will pay for.

Question 91: I hate the idea of talking to the press and speaking at events. Do I have any alternatives at all?

Of course, and this is the fun part. In today's world, all it takes is a good phone along with a bit of editing and you can position your brand (you) and your products (your books) without ever leaving your house. So, if you fall into the shy category or live in remote part of the country, you can still achieve a high level of awareness.

Over the last three years, when I moved from the city to the relative country (a town of 29,000 is country to me), I decided to lay off the traditional marketing and concentrate on the on-line world. While I'd had a Facebook (FB) account for years, Instagram and others, I'd used them for my personal activities, not for my authoring. After I moved, each application went from being discretionary to important. Yet, as I was to quickly learn, important didn't translate to useful for my goals as an author.

The following scorecard represents my own experience with major on-line applications and programs. While other marketing avenues exist, I only have so much time in the day and so went with the dominant platforms.

Table 14. Sarah's marketing program scorecard

Marketing Program	Scorecard	Reason
Instagram	☆☆☆☆	Drives awareness Incredible contacts
YouTube	☆☆☆	Drives views Creates engagement
Facebook	☆☆	Communication tool, general presence
Blogs	☆☆	Reader satisfaction
Book give-away	☆☆☆	Drives views
Cash give-away promo	☆☆	Drives views
Discount deals- eBooks	☆☆☆☆	Drives sales*

❖ More on this in Chapter Nine.

So, what does awareness really amount to?

In Table 14, you can see that the majority of results fall into the branding activities. In plain terms, that means I am reinforcing my brand as an author, and as a part of that, I use these platforms to do three things:

1. Continually keep my name and face out there as a reminder of who I am and what I do.
2. Repeat my author promise, to deliver uplifting, motivational content that's fast-paced, sexy but clean (fiction) and for non-fiction, motivational, successful tips on various subjects.
3. Encourage sales through notices of deals, programs and the like.

Question 92: What is the best philosophy to have when it comes to spending money on marketing my book?

Start out small, test the marketing program, assess the results then budget for a larger effort.

After spending $2,500 on Facebook advertising and other marketing programs and selling less than 100 books, I stopped the programs. However, while the efforts were a complete financial bomb, they paid dividends that couldn't be monetized.

For instance, people found me through on-line social media programs that I would never have met in "real life." One such person, Chuck Pryor, is the radio producer for the Joel Osteen Program. He found me on Instagram (apparently, my motorcycle shots hooked him). He has now produced thirteen radio shows for me without a fee, simply because he likes my work. That saved me over ten grand.

Through Chuck, I've met and interviewed individuals for my non-fiction books on success. One person is one considered one of the top radio program producers in the country, and another is a former number one country music singer.

All of this came from Instagram. Yes, Instagram. It was free to me, and only required I post pictures and captions. Look at where I spent my money and the return on investment.

Table 15. Primary book marketing options

Medium	Cost	Outcome
Facebook- advertising	$2,500	**Made** $20.00 (barely broke even)
Instagram	0.00	**Sales jump** by 40% in an hour then flatlined again
Cash give-away promo on Instagram	$500.00	**Lost money** – e.g. no evident viral activity or book sales
Book give-away	$50.00	No evident viral activity or book sales[3]. However, qualified, interested readers entered to win.
Discount deals- eBooks	Variable	**Immediate sales**. Within 2 hours of a discount email, sales increased 80%.
Blogs	0.00	**Moderate view spike**, unknown pull-through[4]
Site Aggregator	$99.00	Per book. An aggregator is a single entity that lists your books in multiple places. Views and sales increased 45% by using one aggregator alone.
Reviews- Professional	0.00	**Increased views**, no demonstrative sales increase
Reviews- Reader	0.00	No demonstrative sales increase

So, I reset my expectations about what these marketing programs accomplished (create visibility).

---

[3] Cost of books to print and ship.

[4] This means that the direct correlation between the posting of a blog and the sales of my book can't be validated.

Question 93: What is your number one form of marketing then?

At present, the most impactful form of viral marketing for creating awareness, views and likes for me is Instagram. I can see an immediate, direct correlation between a post of a book cover, the shares and most importantly, the sales. Further, Instagram's ability to press a single button and share the same post with Facebook and Twitter make it a simple, single source of communication.

If you are new to Instagram, there are a few things to consider.

Instagram Author Tips

- **Create a protocol—a time(s) for posting**

The best time to post (as told to me by an Instagram executive who has the numbers) is 9 am PST. It gets the highest views from the East Coast and also overseas traffic. For my IG follower base, I receive the fewest Follows on Monday and Tuesday in the am, the most Likes from European followers on Friday am PST and Sunday evening. If I draw conclusions from the numbers, it appears European followers look first thing in the morning. So, my personal data points are different from the norm apparently. Track and follow your own results and adjust accordingly.

- **Use a dependable format**

By this, I mean that posting specific things, on a regular basis, has proven (in my case) to dramatically increase interaction and followers. In my first version on Instagram, I posted random things about my life—cooking, travels, quotes and kids. It was a lackluster response but then I didn't really care because it was a replacement for Instant Messenger, not an author platform. After two months of watching the Instagram accounts of other authors, I realized I was missing the boat. I shut down my account and started up another one (using my middle initial this time because I'd already taken my other name!) and decided to "go author," out of the gate.

My sister, an avid reader and awesome critic, suggested I rotate the types of images I used to be both visually appealing and relevant to my authoring. I took her advice and my numbers started to go up at a predictable, regular rate, about 8.3 followers a day.

- **Don't use bots**. Get real people, real followers, real loyalty

These are real followers, versus the kind that you pay a service to attract. If you aren't familiar with this, a paying service uses automatic bots to follow, like and comment on the IG sites of strangers. It helps you automatically build your Instagram account.

You can also purchase followers and likes directly, through other service providers. It builds your statistics very quickly but I recommend against this approach. Anyone who taps on an account can see the individuals following you are fake accounts, with only a handful of posts and information. It kills your credibility, and much is written about people who use fake accounts. Take your time and do it right. Your readers will track you down and be a part of your community.

- **Establish the right presence and follower base**

As I mentioned, my first iteration of an Instagram account was for me personally, not for my authoring world. When I changed gears and posted more author-related posts, with books and promos, my followers dropped by 2,000 people in about three months from over 6,000. But it started to grow back up gradually. As a friend in the marketing world told me, "They are the people who are actually interested in your books, not just you."

In other words, the new followers were self-identifying: they wanted my author-related content.

➢ **Loyalty, not numbers**

Compared to celebrities, 6,000 followers is miniscule, so I looked up three authors I read, who have had 3-5 NYT bestselling books. Then I looked for their Instagram accounts. One didn't have an IG account at all, and the other two did. Of those, one had just under 1,300 followers and the other about 700. Compared to those two women, my following was rather large.

I dug deeper, comparing my IG account against of the two other (better known) authors. A few things jumped out:

1. **Overuse of a single type of photo**, be it selfies, travel, food or the like. It needs to be varied, but not overly so. Mix it up.
2. **Lack of quotes**. My quotes are shared and used a lot, and the tags of inspiration, motivation, and the like are often searched. On my IG, I intermingle my quotes with those of others. The world is full of wonderful quotes and they should and could be shared.
3. **Activity**. Three posts a day are considered optimal by a lot of "marketing experts," but some weeks, when I only post one

image, I get a ton more likes. Viewers can be fatigued with over-posting.

When talking with a marketing specialist who has headed major brands such as Coke and regularly signs celebrities and public figures for campaigns, he gave me a few more data points:

1. It's better to have 400 than 4,000 followers and ensure those individuals are active and engaged, because they are the true purchasers of your product.
2. The more focused your message, the fewer followers you will get, which is a good thing! You want qualified, invested followers, not bots that will follow and unfollow you.
3. IG accounts with distinct "vibes" stand out. Don't be the same as everyone else, be different. Be as original in your IG account as you are with your writing.
4. Attractive people have a higher follower count, but a far lower engagement (e.g. people click on you less, they don't comment very often etc.) Conversely, physically unattractive people who don't share photos of themselves, but instead focus on content, have a higher, more loyal follower base. Implication: looks attract short-term, flighty, non-loyal followers. Real content=real followers.
5. Causes attract *the most* loyal followers (e.g. pitbull shelters) who are the most engaged (number of times clicked, length of time on the site).
6. Regardless of the number of followers, if you have a pull-

through on any program (like a give-away) that results in more than 1% of people who sign up, you are doing really, really well. To put this in context, 1-3% is the average response rate for really good direct mail campaign that has three rounds.

To prove this out, my first (and only) cash give away of $500 on Instagram resulted in 6 participants out of nearly 4,300 followers. And all the entrants had to do was take a picture of my book, post it and tag me. Repeat: only six followers bothered to enter—for $500! That means only .0012 of my total followers. Wow. Not only that, but it didn't go viral, as I'd hoped, nor did it produce demonstrable sales increase.

Question 94: If it's not increasing my book sales, what's the best way to use Facebook?

Instead of expecting FB to generate sales, consider it a branding and communication tool, particularly for older readers.

- Post links to your blogs, which can be on Goodreads if you don't have your own website yet, or post from your website.
- Post references to articles or other fun resources relevant to your book.
- Post notices of giveaways or other programs you are running for your book.
- Give updates on all your forthcoming press, media and other events you are holding.

A failed experiment

When I first started actively using FB, I thought knew my target customer for my women's fiction was the 35-50 yr. old female crowd. I signed up for an advertising program, set the target audience, and the dollar amount I was prepared to spend. Because this was an experiment, I set the budget for $250 increments.

The first round yielded lots of views and clicks to the purchase page, but not enough sales to meet the expenditure. The second $250, I modified the language, adjusted the target audience (made it broader), and still, few purchases. This continued for eight weeks, and before every campaign, I adjusted the elements of the advertising campaign, from the demographics to the range. Week after week, the statistics were the same. Barely enough sales to pay for the program but lots of views and clicks. If I counted the hours spent on the program, I was in the hole. My conclusion is that paying FB for advertising is a waste of time for authors, particularly those starting out.

Question 95: Can I leverage my personal Facebook page to my author page?

Yes, to a degree. Public pages are followed by people who have an interest in that subject. Not all relatives, friends or church members are going to like or even care about what you write.

If your desire is to jump start your author FB page using your personal page, then get creative. Design a program that can get you a lot of views without spending a ton of money on advertising.

- **Contests**

My first program to build up Facebook followers was a contest I concocted to name the book that eventually was called *Chambers.* I went from 6 to nearly 400 followers in less than two weeks. It was easy to do, and compared to total amount of $2,500 I spent on FB, highly cost effective.

The contest details:

- Announced a naming contest and grand prize (diamond hoop earrings. Macy's was having a 60% off sale so I picked up a pair for $120).
- Created a special chambersseries gmail account for submissions.
- FB users could submit as many names as they liked, and this allowed me to know what had been submitted by whom (and in what order)
- Set a deadline.
- I used one of the FB apps that allows for surveys.
- I modeled the process after the Final Four. I divided the names into a bunch of individual checklist surveys. One by one, I posted the surveys, allowing 48 hours for selection.
- I took the top two in each survey, reducing it again, and then once again.
- The final four names were posted for 48 hours of voting.
- I had a run-off with the final two names.

- The winner was announced and results posted immediately.

Beyond the number of followers, I learned that the contest itself had gone viral because many of the participants wanted the earrings so badly that they were getting their friends and anyone they knew to look at my FB page and vote for their submitted name!

➢ **Facebook, blogs and links**

As I can't be bothered to spend hours on FB, I limit my postings to the four bullet points I listed previously, but maximize my social media efforts by reposting Instagram pics that I think are relevant for my Facebook followers.

Using the analytics built into my website, I can see where the viewers are from and where they spend the most time. It's how I know that nearly half my followers/viewers/readers are from outside the United States. It's not surprising, as a number of my books are set abroad. My personal interests, travel etc., also touch on life beyond America.

The analytics also tell me which blogs get the heaviest traffic and how much time is spent on my site. I adjust the topics I post according to that data, and it has increasingly improved my traffic. I used to put up a site counter which logged the number of visitors, but took this off when I had to change my site two times and the counter had to start over. It was fun to track though—and may be something you want to consider.

Question 96: Does the number of followers on FB count

then?

Count to who? If you base your happy factor, self-esteem or success as an author on the number of likes you have or the total follower count on FB, you might want to have a valium handy, because people are fickle, likes and follows are temporary. Be clear why and how FB "counts," to you.

FB is worth it for views and impressions, but it's also plays an important role as a communication vehicle in the publishing world.

In one instance, I had a translator from Poland track me down and find me through Facebook when she had questions regarding the Polish translation of *Chambers*. The publisher and my agent at the time hadn't responded, and she was on a deadline and anxious. I helped her out and within a week we had gone through all her questions.

My advice on Facebook is have a FB author page but manage it wisely so it doesn't consume your time and take away from writing.

One way to maximize your social media efforts is to establish a master account from Instagram. Just before you officially post a picture, you have an option to post it simultaneously to other pages you manage, such as Twitter, Facebook and more. You can set this up at any time. That way, you post once and it is shared and viewed multiple times.

Question 97: What are book ratings? Do I need them and do they have an impact on sales?

I'll admit, until three months ago, the phrase book ratings had never been raised by anyone in my editorial world or my agent. Yet, it gained a new importance when the producer of my radio show, *Author Straight Talk*, called me one day with news about book ratings.

Here's what happened. After he finished reading my latest women's fiction book, up popped a book suggested by Amazon. He looked up the author, saw that she had a million blog readers a month (literally, one million) and had sold a million copies of her two, independently (not-self published) books.

> Once a book is rated, and validated by the Book Cave system (with its own listing and link), then the book can be listed on any one of these sites that require a book to be rated.

I looked her up, and sure enough, both statistics are promoted on her site. Investigating deeper, it turns out she belongs to a particular religion, and where did readers of this devout (and well-known) religious group find her? Websites specifically geared for fiction authors of that religion, and those books required a rating to be listed on the sites.

How ratings boosted awareness and visibility

I then learned that the website in question, as well as a great many other Christian and religious organizations not affiliated with any particular sect, use book ratings offered by

MyBookCave.com/MyBookRatings. Once a book is rated and validated by the Book Cave rating system (with its own listing and link), then the book can be listed on any one of these religious sites.

It took about three weeks from the time I filled out the forms before my books were approved until I could start listing on various sites. In order to even list your books, you need to a) have already gone through the book rating system for each and every book and b) have the link and description ready to input.

The sales impact was noticeable (about a 2% difference) in the first two weeks. When other websites started listing my books (again, thanks to the ratings that were in place), **sales doubled again**. Noticing the change, I then applied a few of the other promotions for book give away and discount deals.

Whether it was the listings themselves or the fact I was using a holistic approach to creating demand, I can't be sure. I suspect the latter, because it's all a compounding effect for the reader.

What to do:

1. Go to MyBookCave, establish an account.
2. Once you have an account, you can submit your books on mybookratings.
3. Submit individual listings for each book.
4. This requires a complete audit of the book in various categories.
5. Wait for the link (about two weeks). If it isn't sent to you, follow-up with customer support.
6. Once you have the link, go back to the site

requesting/requiring the book rating.

7. Fill out and submit and wait for approval and listing.

Question 98: What about paying for reviews?

If you are unfamiliar with a paid review, it's the practice of paying an entity a set amount to have a "professionally written review" of your book. Generally, services run between $200-400 per review, wherein the book is read by three qualified "editors." I've always wondered if these are, in fact, an editor in the way it's typically defined or simply avid readers. Regardless, the book is read and a single review (not three) is generated and sent to you. URL links are also delivered by some companies so it appears to be an independent third-party.

However, it takes very little effort to click on the link and determine the source of the review. The next question is: why would you pay for a review? It's because a very small percentage of books published by traditional houses even get reviewed by a mainstream publication. Very few, if any, books published by independent entities or self-published get reviewed at all.

Ironically, that's why *PW* created its own for-pay review organization: they get paid money by you, the author, to review a book that they won't cover in their main publication.

Readers are smart. They know which individuals and organizations give paid reviews, and so are likely to discount whatever is written (like I do), and then end up going to recognized entities such as a major newspaper or *Publishers Weekly* (PW).

Personally, I don't pay for reviews, but I know authors who do, and the number of paid reviews hasn't dramatically impacted the sales of the books.

Question 99: Does the number of reviews make a difference in book sales?

Yes. According to my industry insiders, and my own experience, the threshold number of reader reviews required to have an impact on sales is twenty. Below twenty reader reviews, prospective buyers assume the reviewers are "friends and family," which might may or may not be the truth.

Like so many other elements of the authoring world, I disputed this fact and ignored it until I experienced it over and over again with each one of my books. Then, when each book hit twenty reviews, the sales went up dramatically. Interestingly, the number of reviews didn't increase in accordance with sales. Publisher statistics given to me indicate that for every 100 readers, less than 1% write a review.

If the author isn't actively marketing or promoting the book, readers and reviews are truly organic, and the first twenty reviews can take months to gather. After six months, however, if readers aren't buying the book, or they are and not giving it rave reviews, don't worry. Keep writing.

Question 100: How do you get reviews?

For fiction, I use a few different approaches, but only for a short period of time, say two weeks. Usually, the combined activities yield about ten reviews. That seems to be enough for the reviews to increase on their own.

A few ways to jump start reviews for fiction:

- Offer free eBooks on your author Facebook page- for the first ten respondents. Usually, only 3-5 will actually download the book and 1-2 will post a review.
- Add free books here through magnets. If you haven't heard of, or used magnets, it is a free link provided by MyBookCave that gives authors the ability to distribute their work for free, either in epub or mobi format. This is a lifesaver, because many authors were using Amazon's egift feature for distributing eBooks to potential reviewers.
- Offer discount eBooks or print book to your network, blog or social media platforms. Again, the same numbers apply as the above.
- Join an author's group, such as on Goodreads, well in advance of your book's release. When the book is completed, and you have an Advance Review Copy (ARC) available, announce it to the author's group and offer a free copy.

In case you didn't notice, thousands of reviews on Amazon were removed the summer of 2017. These were reviews that were the result of e-gifts. In the past, publishers would send out printed copies to editors, reporters, bloggers etc. With the advent of eBooks, it became the norm to send eBooks—it was faster and far less costly. Unfortunately, Amazon decided to treat these reviews differently than their print counterpart. So, all of us authors, independent publishers and even mainstream publishers, suffered when the reviews were pulled. For *Chambers* alone, I had hundreds of reviews pulled down. 200 or so were the result of giveaways I'd provided to attendees to launch events, such as television show audiences. I elected not to spend the money or effort on rebuilding years' worth of reviews. They will come (again) but it will take a while, especially with the statistic that only 1 review is written for every 100 books read.

For non-fiction, I employ the advance review process I've always used, which in summary, is to send ARC's to a list of peers, associates and acquaintances in the industry I'm writing about.

A few tips on reviews for non-fiction:

- When you are interviewing the subjects for your non-fiction book, ask if they have a handful of individuals with prominent positions in their field.
- Identify that when the time comes, you may come back and ask for contact details.
- When the book is nearing completion of editing and layout, re-contact the subjects, and ask for personal introductions 2-3

individuals. These people will be/are friends of the person you have interviewed and are likely to be interested in the topic matter. They will also be more likely to help out their peer, associate or friend, who is quoted in the book.

- Ask your interviewee for a personal introduction; usually an e-mail introduction is best.
- Identify to the interviewee that you only desire a one or two sentence quote on the content of the book, and its value to the target market.
- Offer to provide the person with a signed copy of the final, printed book.
- Once agreed upon, offer to send the PDF copy of the manuscript. Provide the individual with a desired timeframe (thirty days is optimal, but know that most will wait until the very last minute).
- Assemble the quotes, re-approve the quote with the provider to ensure accuracy, and put this on the inside flap, or outside cover of the book, as well as your marketing material.

Question 101: Any tips on getting back of the book quotes for my fiction?

Certainly. Some of the most interesting and compelling quotes are those considered "book jacket cover quotes," provided by another author. This is intimidating to nearly all aspiring—and published—authors I know. It requires a bit of confidence, yes, but look at it this way. The worst that can happen is you will get turned down, which means you were no worse off than you were before you asked the question.

I'll make it a little easier for you by providing a few in-roads to reaching another author.

- About the same time you have the ARC in hand, make a wish list of authors. Local authors, within your state and then region. If you have national-level authors you believe would be ideal, put them down as well.
- If you have an agent or publisher, look at their existing list of authors and create a sub-list. Request their help in soliciting a review.
- If you are self-published, network within the community and see if you can make connections. Be brave and call up the local editor of the newspaper (ideally who has covered the target author) and ask for an introduction.
- Author networks, on line or in person. If you are an author on Goodreads, you should join an author's group. Participate. Be helpful. Be patient and be willing to help others before you need assistance yourself. When the time comes, you contact those authors in your network for an advance reading and review.
- Your Goodreads followers. I used this approach for my recent book, and out of fourteen followers, five responded with strong interest in certain genres, and two one that went above my expectations, and read all my books. What's in it for them? Free books and the association with a real, live,

author. You would be surprised how much this last aspect means to readers.

- Teachers (English, business etc.) will often know the local authors who give of their time to help out at the college level. This means the author may be inclined to help you. Again, don't be shy. Ask the professor for an introduction. This may even turn up a discussion with the professor about reading your book as well, which could result in an early review.

About the email itself

Compose a friendly email introducing yourself and contains the salient information about your book. Genre, high-level storyline, publisher, release date, etc. Other details, such as where the endorsement will be used, when you'd like the quote by, and the like, should also be included.

Several first-time authors I know started a rapport with authors on social media, either through Goodreads, or even Facebook accounts. They initiated contact months before the eventual request was going to come about. By that time, the author was familiar with the aspirations of their reader (the aspiring author) and genuinely wanted to help out. This takes a bit of forethought, but ultimately doesn't require anything other than your time and attention.

Question 102: What role does a publicist play in marketing the book?

A good publicist will do the following :

➢ **Get reviews**

Help put your book in front of the right publications for reviews (if, and only if, your book is published by a mainstream publisher). These are members of the media, professional editors/reporters or bloggers. A handful of organizations will review books by self-published authors, but they have very strict and defined criteria. If you don't want to spend the time and money researching and sending the pitch letters, your publicist will do this for you.

➢ **Assemble the editorial calendar for articles**

An editorial calendar is a list of target publications that will cover you or your book.

➢ **Pitch the editors/writers within the editorial calendar**

This is typically a nine-month effort and needs to be budgeted as such. Monthlies or quarterlies are long-lead publications. Those need to be pitched six months before the article will appear. Then the publicist pitches the monthlies, then as the launch date nears, the weeklies, local radio shows and television shows.

Within "the pitch" is the reason why you are interesting, unique, topical and your book is the next best thing. Each story pitch must be tailored to that specific publication, the topic list on the editorial calendar and even the writer preferences and style of writing.

It's a big job, and if you can find someone who will work for monthly fee of less than $1,250, consider yourself blessed. Most independent PR consultants will be in the $2-3,000 range, and that's only if they have a stable of authors or clients that are giving them scale. If you are in a big city, you are likely looking at $5-10K for a short and finite project (that's the total amount you would pay).

If you are anticipating a public relations program of six months or more, you are looking at this amount *per month.* Most PR professionals won't take on a project for less than 9 months, because pitching and placing is only the front half of the job. The last and most critical part of the publicity process is following up with each writer and editor to ensure the story hasn't stalled or gotten deprioritized, the pictures or follow up shots are included and when the article will appear.

This is a very detailed task, and one that carries with it a bit of risk. Your article can be shunted for a more news-worthy and topical item. The article might not be as complete or in-depth as you would like. The reporter may get a few details incorrect, or worst of all, the review or positioning of the book could be unfavorable. These are all possible outcomes, and it would be no fault of your publicist.

Sales not guaranteed

Now let's talk about sales from the resulting press, assuming it's all goes to plan. It's relevant to put this here, in the marketing section, rather than the sales, because public relations forwards awareness but not necessarily sales.

Press and the printed articles fall into the category of branding. **You are creating awareness and demand for the product, your book, but that isn't necessarily going to translate into tons of sales.** I could recite studies from consumer products companies who have spent billions on marketing campaigns but I'll drill it down to this:

In the early days of a campaign, you are positioning the brand. You are creating name awareness, so when a person mentions your name, Suzy James, the consumer nods their head and says, yeah, I've heard of her. As the campaign progresses, additional elements are added. Suzy James writes time travel sci-fi. Yes, the consumer responds, time travel sci-fi. If a campaign has this level of effectivity, then the marketing manager and publicist are jumping for joy. But the author isn't. Beyond having an improved sense of self and getting recognized at the local grocery story, sales have not changed.

Let me share an example of this example happening to me.

When *Chambers* launched, I appeared on three Seattle television shows, a secondary talk show, and had major, front page profiles in five publications in different cities as I'd previously mentioned, the oversize, full color pictorials bound to result in sales.

The total sales resulting from these thousands of impressions? Less than fifty.

We were all stymied. Mystified. Pissed off. What in the world had happened?

It didn't take long until we took a look at the demographics for all the television programs. The audiences were full of women, over the age of forty, and from talking to the audience afterward and between breaks, there was lots of grey hair and grandmas. The same held true for the readers of the newspapers, a demographic that are traditionally older, because younger generations (anything below 45) are reading news on the Internet or phone.

This would have been perfect for my women's contemporary

fiction books, but I was still four years away from writing those!

Chambers was the book I was promoting, a young adult time travel adventure novel. The publicist couldn't be blamed—well, she could and I'll name her. Me. I had pitched all those stories, and I must say, the coverage was fantastic. But the audience didn't translate to the purchasing of the book, for their grandkids, kids or anyone else.

The summary: great press, wrong audience, no sales.

Since that time and now, the number of print publications has dwindled significantly, giving less editorial space to the same amount of (or more) stories. That's a contributing reason why authors and all marketing managers flock to the on-line communities to market and promote their products.

Question 103: I wrote a novel and my agent is telling me it's not "in trend" anymore. Do I scrap it and write to the current trend?

"There is no such thing as writing to a trend," said one editor of a top-five publishing house who wishes to remain anonymous. "You are either ahead of a trend, which means no publisher wants to take a chance on it, or you are behind the trend, which means the next 3-4 years in the schedule is already full of books waiting to be published."

The author is caught in a Catch-22.

On one hand, it's tempting to jump on the rising wave of a new genre. The reality is that mainstream publishers schedule books out 24-48 months. By the time the general public—you and me—know about it and are purchasing the books, it's too late to hop on the surfboard and ride the wave.

One day, during the whole Stephenie Meyer vampire-paranormal frenzy, I was talking with Peter about the buzz among agents. I was specifically trying to get the inside dirt on what was going to be trendy. He was lamenting that everyone one was sending him. "Yet another vampire or zombie novel, some quite good," he added, but the publishers simply weren't interested.

"What do they want?" I asked.

"They don't know, not yet anyway. Just not that."

Question 104: What if I'm writing in a genre that doesn't exist—or at least not exactly. Is that impossible?

Not impossible, it's just a harder road for your publishing journey. Think Ann Rice, who created the dark vampire genre. She self-published her first book and sold her copies on a street corner. (I tried that, by the way, at Pike Place Market, in Seattle. Number of copies sold: two.) Rice had the fortitude to keep going back, graduating to street markets until word of mouth caught on and she eventually got picked up by a mainstream publisher.

The category of "legal thriller" didn't exist before John Grisham wrote *The Firm.* Grisham hawked his first books at local libraries, back in the day when an author could bring in donuts and coffee and give his books away (most libraries have banned this practice).

Amanda Hocking is credited with furthering the "paranormal" category and some industry professionals attribute the entire category to her work. After self-publishing eBooks and selling hundreds of thousands of copies, she was picked up by a mainstream publisher and given a seven-figure advance.

The message here is that creating a category does happen, you just have to be aware of the challenges you will face.

Question 105: Do I need to keep writing in the same genre?

When you are starting out, I'd encourage you to try your hand at several genres and see what feels more natural. When you settle on a genre that feels right to you, then explore writing with different points of view. I dislike first person (both reading and writing it), but at the request of the movie studio, I promised to try. Turns out, I write well enough in the first person that the studio optioned the entire series based upon the first book. Who knew? Now, even though I don't prefer first person, when I have a book where it makes sense for the character, I use it.

Question 106: If I create my own genre, what are the challenges I'll face?

The ability to give a one-line description that people will understand is just the beginning of your challenges. A close second is the resulting agent opposition, publisher resistance and reader confusion.

> Don't feel bound by one genre or style of writing (first person etc.), but recognize it takes a lot of time to perfect your craft. Become as proficient as possible in that style and genre before adding another.

Think of listing your book. You may not find your new genre, which makes it hard to adequately position the book and challenging for the reader to get a true understanding of the content.

Genres and category-related issues extend to promotions such as book giveaways and alerts. As you are given only the primary genres to choose from, your targeted message won't resonate with a broad audience. This translates to lower impressions with your target market and, of course, lower sales.

Editorial services are a second challenge. I mentioned earlier; strategic editors specialize in genres. They are familiar with the typical flow, style and structure of what makes a bestseller in a genre. Your goal is to locate an editor in your genre, but if it's new, how are you (or the editor you speak with) going to know what will work best? No one likes a failure, and editors are no different. You may have a hard time finding an editor who will take the project on.

Question 107: What are the benefits of a new genre?

Complete and utter literary freedom. You can write what you want, how you want, setting aside all the criteria that authors in set genres must conform to.

Question 108: If I have self-published in a new genre (I've created) and the readers love the book, then why am I getting so much pushback from potential mainstream publishers?

This is a really good problem to have! It means you have sold enough copies in any form to warrant attention. The downside is that by virtue of being original and different, you don't fit nicely into any of the business operational categories.

Every system and promotional tool, from the catalogues to the sales reps, the layouts and the reporting, all have codes assigned and ways of managing a category and sub-category within a genre. So, as much as a publisher or excited agent will say they are looking for the next best thing, the very nature of the entire infrastructure is dead set against actually producing such a book.

The operational costs and infrastructure investment is huge. Imagine paranormal comes on the scene, but the graphics department has no idea what covers will sell most. The editors aren't sure what style is going to be the most popular, and the sales woman/man visiting the retail bookstores has never used the word before and is pitching a book that may be wildly successful or a spectacular flop. That salesperson has the challenging job of convincing the book buyer to take a chance on something brand new and many decline. The only reason some of the book buyers will take a chance is because most publishers give generous terms for credit (a year and half to pay the publisher, for thc book) or get a refund from the publisher for books that have gone unsold.

Sales

CHAPTER HIGHLIGHTS

- *Pricing*
- *Programs*
- *Agents and imprints*

Obstacles don't have to stop you. If you run into a wall, don't turn around and give up. Figure out how to climb it, go through it, or work around it.

Michael Jordan

Selling your book is the pinnacle of months or years' worth of effort. If you are fortunate enough to have a mainstream publisher, the book price will be set without your involvement. Self-published authors will set the price of the book, based on the costs of the printing and distribution entity, who have baseline costs. You, the author, determine the retail price of the book.

This chapter covers pricing strategies and offers. One of the first questions is: How do I set the price? Yet this is just one of the factors in book sales. Programs and promotions factor into increasing sales, and then if you are successful, you may attract the attention of a bonified agent. Who knows? You may be approached by a television producer who wants to option your book.

If those are the upsides of sales, the downside is the book isn't selling at all. This brings us full-circle back to the fear, uncertainty and doubt of being an author. It's a fact that even bestselling authors must confront: not all books are hits, just as not all movies by an Oscar winning director are loved. It will happen, so be prepared.

Question 109: I'm really naïve about pricing and conventions. What are the basics I should know about pricing?

If you are a first-time author, I'll share a few basic authoring guidelines and statistics you may want to keep in mind.

For printed books:

- A novella is typically 220 pages
- A novel is typically 325 pages or more
- Cookbooks and romance sell more in the printed form
- Hardcover books for trade and reference outsell paperback copies but don't necessarily give higher margins
- Certain genres and formats have "typical" ranges for pricing:
  - 6 x 9 books range between $11.95-$16.95. The difference

is the page count, which changes the margins. You will find that a 325 book, on average, will be between $11.95-$14.95, a price point that sells best

- o Novellas under 220 pages will be in the sub-$10.00 range: $7.95 or less is optimal for sales.
- o Hardbound books in the 225-250 page count range between $14.95-$17.95, but sell best if below $15.00.
- o Hardbound books in the 250-350 page count range between $17.95-$22.95, and generally sell the best if priced no higher than $21.95.
- o Printed books, hardbound, or hardbound with a flap, range up to $29-$32.00 but these are high-page count reference books.

For eBooks:

- eBooks in the romance categories are the highest/swiftest selling and are priced "to move" the best at $1.99. Series sell best when book one is .99 cents, with the price increased with each subsequent book.
- Action adventure, sci-fi and suspense books are the highest priced eBooks on average in the fiction category--$4.99 or more, if self-published. The rational is that these books are longer and the readers will be more inclined to pay a higher price for those categories.
- The trend on pricing eBooks is to stay within a 30% range of the print book. If you have a print book for $12.95, the

eBook priced is going to be around the $7-9 range. If you factor for discounts or promotions, you are then really selling your book for $6.99.

Question 110: What are good pricing strategies for a first-time author?

Lots of philosophies exist on this, and because I feel like I've tried them all, I'll share with you my experience (and other authors who provided their data and results) of what sells the best.

Table 16. Pricing conventions

Book	Page count	Price point
First time eBook	<250 pages	.99
First time eBook	>250-300 pages	$1.99
First time eBook	>350 pages	$2.99
Second eBook	>350 pages	$3.99
Third eBook	>350 pages	$4.99
Imprint (softcover)	<250 pages	$7.95-9.95 fiction $12.05 non-fiction
Imprint (softcover)	>325 pages	$11.95+ fiction $12.95+ non-fiction
Imprint (softcover)	>450 pages	$14.95+ fiction

When you are starting out your pricing strategy, you may want to think about the word convention. A convention is a framework that you will use time and again, which ensures consistency. A few well-publicized pricing strategies are being used by many authors. One is to lower the price of the first eBook in a series to $.99. Then increase the second book to $1.99 and the third to $2.99, where it holds steady. I tried this strategy, and I know of four other authors who did the same. The result? No material difference in the sales of the book.

Another strategy is to give the first book away free, hook the reader into the series and then raise the price. This is known as the freemium model. Free until it moves to pay, or premium model.

Outside the publishing world, this is known as a loss-leader. You take a loss on the first product, (the first book), build the market and then raise the price.

The issue with this is two-fold. **First, it undervalues your work**, and studies have proven that people unconsciously equate free with poor quality. That sets you, your brand and your product at a disadvantage. Your time and product are worth something. **Second, and equally important, it gives you nowhere to go for a book promotion**. You need to have a set price in order to give a discount. If your starting point is free, you have just excluded your book from hundreds of promotional opportunities.

A few other data points. When I listed my eBooks at .99, sales were slow and quite modest. When I raised it to $1.99, sales increased and were more frequent. I thought back to the standard pricing philosophies that hinged on the notion of price=value.

You can imagine what I did. I raised the price to $2.99 and bingo. Sales increased again and remained steady.

Finding the balance

If you look at my prices today, you will see my pricing

convention for eBooks is a price point of between $3.99 or $5.99 for fiction and non-fiction respectively. Believe it or not, I kept raising the price to the threshold that made sense in comparison to the print book. I try to stay within the thirty percent range of the print book for my women's contemporary fiction. Sometimes the eBook price should be a little higher, but I then put on my 'reader hat.' I don't like paying more than $7.00 for a fiction book, and rarely (as in, never) do it. If I'm going to pop that much for an eBook, I'm going to buy the print, because honestly, I like print books better.

Raise the eBook price to the threshold consistent for the genre and approximately 30% of the imprint version.

That philosophy has paid lots of dividends. It turns out that $4.99 seems to the be threshold that readers will pay for women's fiction, because my sales evened out. Note I didn't say diminished, they are holding steady. The most interesting thing about this pricing experiment with women's fiction is that I noticed a huge uptick in the purchase of the paperback versions (I don't offer my women's fiction in hardcover). The margin is plentiful on the imprint, so it's been a nice, unexpected result.

Fiction genres and non-fiction

Now I'll give you the *Chambers* example. The price/value equation holds true in this genre. The lower the price, the fewer the sales, the higher the price, the higher the sales. Also, this is a 450 page book, and a "saga," to use a phrase often applied to five-book series. The eBook on this is $3.99, which is only a dollar higher in price, but it immediately identifies the book is longer, weightier and perhaps more complex in the content (which is, in fact, true). The print version however, is in the $12.95 and on up range for paperback and hardcover. It has been surprising to learn that the eBook and hardcover far outsell the imprint. This suggests that the readers in this genre are going to either consume it quickly on a device, or want to keep it around on the shelf for quite some time.

Non-fiction is a different beast entirely. Originally, I priced all my books in the convention described for fiction. Then I took note of the non-fiction books I was buying for my own reading. The eBook prices were identical to the imprint version. Further, rarely did the publisher offer a discount on the eBook version if the imprint had been purchased. They got me, the reader, coming and going.

> Many non-fiction trade books are priced identically. Use your judgement if you want to lower the eBook price, but have confidence that straight across pricing is considered standard.

I decided to split the difference and give a little bit of a discount, but not much. I view my non-fiction titles as having a long shelf life and deep content, e.g. having a higher value. With that in mind, I reduced the eBook of the *Sue Kim Authorized Biography*. The other books in my library are also slightly discounted. Do you recall what I wrote earlier, about publishers knowing that non-fiction reference books are often purchased in both print and eBook formats? My numbers indicate that this is the case, because the sales are nearly identical on the day, week and month.

Question 111: Should I write for the reader or myself?

This question was originally posed to me by a user on Instagram, who I texted with a request for his email, since the answer was longer than my thumbs could handle. The question has an answer for non-fiction and another for fiction.

Non-fiction is simple. The author has a specific audience in mind: entrepreneurs, small businesses, sales people, or another target audience who has a need the author is going to address. The author is writing exclusively to that audience, both in language and content. The publisher has read the author's proposal, knows exactly how many potential book buyers are in that category, and has estimated the percentage of those potential buyers who will be reached and will purchase the book.

The publishers of those books have those audiences nailed, and as this was the case with my non-fiction trade titles, I was literally told the POV I'd use, the writing style and given a format designed to appeal to the audience. They had decades of data showing what would sell and wouldn't, down to the number of words on the page, the number of graphical elements and total page count.

Writing in that category was hard for me. While I love the content, writing the book was like working on a textbook. Important but dry, the final product was accurate but lacking all the wonderful, horrible stories of failure because of space considerations.

Fiction is entirely different. You, the author, must create a story that is genuine to your voice and perspective, one that is ultimately believable to the reader.

> In non-fiction, you are writing to, and for a specific audience. In fiction, you are writing for yourself. Please that singular audience, and you will likely please many others.

I shared the story about "finding my voice" after a series of tragic events, so I'm not going to go through that again. The outcome is what I want to emphasize. Beyond the fact my agent loved the book and my library of books in that genre have sold well, the books were written by me, for me. I actually like reading my own work. If I'd not sold a single one, it would have been a perfectly acceptable outcome because I had written what I myself wanted to read.

To the non-fiction writer, I say: write to the audience with the appropriate subject. To the fiction writer, I say: write what pleases you. It will be the most authentic, fulfilling experience you can have, and the reader will be satisfied.

Question 112: How long before I become famous, and will this help my sales?

The reason this question is included in the Sales chapter is because many aspiring authors, myself included, mistakenly believe the visibility translates to sales (see previous chapter!). You can be famous in your small community and treated like a Rockstar. But does fame translate to sales? I've already related my own experience, so will share another.

Decades ago, a reclusive author could live in a remote location, receive positive book reviews, become rich and reluctantly famous. I recall that Oprah got a media shy author on her show, one who had not given a single interview in thirty years (forgive me for not recalling his name. I never read his work).

"Why have you refused to give interviews or promote your book?" she asked.

"I never had to," the man replied. "My books sold on their own."

Those days are long gone. Today, authors must work hard on the business of authoring. So, fame is nice and may get you the initial buzz, similar to the opening weekend of a movie, but no amount of advertising is going to get a viewer back in the movie theatre seat if the film is a dud.

Question 113: What about YouTube as a selling tool?

YouTube is a means to get yourself and your content to an audience in an immediate, visual fashion. Publishing insiders tell me that their studies show readers often turn to YouTube to a) get how-to content quicker than reading a book, b) learn know about you, the author, or c) to hear you read your fiction works.

Not all authors want to get behind a camera. Heaven knows after nearly twenty years, I've only done so reluctantly, and that's because I felt I was missing a huge opportunity, particularly for my non-fiction work. Another reason is the financial motivation. YouTube shares revenue earned from advertising that appears before, during and after the videos. Once you reach a threshold of views (it's currently 10,000 but changes all the time), the creator of the video starts to make money.

In the last week alone, I've watched the videos of two different aspiring authors who have created channels on YouTube. Mind you, neither actually have books out, but they are talking about their angst, the process and all sorts of things related to writing in unique ways. Each have built a following of thousands of followers and are surely making money—despite not having a book.

Consider your situation. If you have a smart phone, the ability to edit and post a video here and there of you, your process, your own issues or successes, you can start branding yourself today. You don't have to wait for the book cover to be complete or the manuscript proofed.

I've had two go-arounds with YouTube. Here's what I did wrong the first time out and how I corrected it with version 2.0.

- I named the channel after my first fiction book series.

Mistake. I should have given it my name. I am now in the process of switching it over. The result? I have temporarily lost the ability to use my actual name. Back then, one could register with YouTube with a name. No longer. No, one must get 100 subscribers before YouTube will give you that name in your URL.

➢ Understanding the power of an intro reel.

An introductory video should convey five things: 1) who you are, 2) what you will provide in your channel, 3) how the viewer will benefit, 4) how often you will post, and 5) how they can find/get more information. I only recently got wise to this and will be putting one up shortly. Getting wise means that other authors who use an intro reel notice a dramatic jump in views and subscribers.

Keep the commitment of regular videos. Views happen when the content is relevant or entertaining. Subscribers, on the other hand, only happen when regular videos are uploaded and the viewer is interested in getting notified.

Why are subscribers important? Because you can then monetize (turn into money) a portion of your free subscribers into a paying subscriber base (think Jillian Michaels with free workout videos and then premium videos for pay). You also enjoy a higher percentage of revenue share from advertising.

I've only just begun capitalizing on YouTube in this fashion, so I have no data to share. I can't identify a direct correlation to sales at this point, as it's only been a month with the new YouTube channel.

Question 114: What will creating and managing a YouTube channel cost me?

The answer depends on your acumen, availability and interest in learning YouTube. I'll admit I'm not a visual girl, and this entire process was so painful I basically avoided it for years. That said, it was easy enough, but time consuming, to set up the channel. I paid money to my designer (the same one I use out of Bulgaria) who repurposed the covers of my books for a collage I could use across Instagram, YouTube and my website. So that was done for the bargain basement price of $100. I love a global universe of artists!

For the recording aspect, I use an HD camera by Microsoft which I picked up for about $25.00 at Staples. I attach this to a paper towel holder using a large paperclip, which is set upon a stack of books. No, I'm not kidding. The reason for this was because it was the right height. After purchasing, and returning, three different stands for my phone, I realized they were too short or too tall, so I went basic, and it worked perfectly. For the microphone, I did pop for the $50.00 Samsung mic, that I also put atop four books. This was near enough to capture my audio, but not so close it was included in the filming.

The first few episodes were a little rough. I wasn't used to speaking in front of the camera, as my media days were about a decade ago. That meant reshooting multiple times. However, after a couple of hours, I relaxed, the interviews went more smoothly and we had enough material to edit

Notice I used the word "we?" That's because Chuck Pryor was, and is, the person who interviewed me. The format I chose was different from many other authors I see on YouTube, who start the camera rolling and being talking. This is great, and I have nothing but positive things to say about the format. How could I? Those videos get tens of thousands of views. But I wanted to take a different approach, one where a third-party and myself interacted. Chuck offered to do the task, I took him up on it, and now we have a format that I'll continue to use.

You could take this same approach with anyone you know, a friend, associated, business partner—whomever. The other day, I watched two, twenty-somethings who consider themselves foodies. They literally sit and talk about food. Each video gets about 100,000 views. That's some nice cash in the bank. No fancy camera work. No amazing pictures or music. Just two guys talking about food.

If you got in front of a camera and talked about writing with your best friend, I wonder what magic you could create.

The editing is the biggest time sink of the process. Again, a range of professionalism exists here, from the basic to top of the line. My material is probably on the mid to lower end of the range. My lead-in and exits have moving graphics and some animation with music, which gives it a professional look, but isn't over the top. Could more be done? Absolutely. Will I pay hundreds or thousands of dollars for that extra 10%? Absolutely not. At this point, my YouTube channel isn't making me money, and I don't expect it to do so for some time. It's an awareness generation vehicle that will turn into a revenue generator with enough subscribers. Until then, I'm focusing on the content, which means maximum writing.

Question 115: When and how do book promotions come into play?

Book promotions come in various flavors, so I'll break it down.

- **Giveaways**. You are literally giving away a number of copies, free of charge. These are typically signed copies, sent by you to the recipient, who is the winner of a drawing.
- **Discounts**. You have temporarily discounted your book, usually an eBook, for a period of time, across some, or all of the available platforms, such as Kobo, Amazon etc.
- **Discounts using targeted mailing lists**. This is a pay-for-play program where you offer either a discount or giveaway, and this is announced to a very specific list of potential buyers who have already opted-in (or requested) books in a particular genre(s).

When I began using these programs, I did so in sequential order, and one at a time, so I could see the results.

Question 116: What are the details of a book give-away, and what are the best strategies for giveaways?

The number one benefit of a book give away is the free visibility to a reader who has already self-qualified their interest in a genre.

It works like this: a reader goes to a site offering giveaways, such as Goodreads. You must have an author account (not just a reader account). You fill out the information required, approve an email from Goodreads that verifies you agreed to the conditions, such as sending the books out two weeks upon the end of the giveaway. You must also promise not to contact the recipients at any time, or you will be reported. (Goodreads provides you the name and physical address to send the signed copies directly). Once you are approved by Goodreads, then the promotion starts on the day you have specified.

Question 117: I don't have a ton of money to be purchasing books, then turning around and sending them to recipients. Any advice?

Yes. Prioritize your funds and save the fifty dollars it's going to cost you and do it. An average imprint cost on either CreateSpace or Nook is about five dollars. You can afford to purchase three books and then send those books to winners.

For this fifty-dollar investment, you are going to get thousands of views to your giveaway, in addition to those individuals who register. Additionally, my data suggests that quite a few of the readers can't (or don't want to) wait to read your book, and this results in sales. On top of all of this, many of these hopeful winners add the book to their 'to-read' list.

At this stage in my career, I'm highly dubious of any promo or giveaway and the projected results. Still, this version of the Goodreads giveaway is free, so I figured, why not? I'll see what happens. (Two other giveaway programs exist, which cost $119 and $599 premium per book as of this writing).

Question 118: Can you show me how to run a giveaway promotion and what I should expect?

Absolutely.

A few notes on my approach. First, I ignored the recommendation by Goodreads to run a 30-day minimum timeframe. One data point on purchasing habits is that buyers wait until the last minute. With that in mind, I created two short and one long-term periods for the giveaways. Second, I ignored the recommendation to offer a single copy of a book. I went with five. Lots has been written about the exclusivity factor of offering one copy. Ok, I buy that to a degree. At the same time, I paid a lot for statistics while working in corporate marketing to know that if the odds are so low of winning, many potential entrants don't even bother. Lastly, when looking at the numbers of entrants for giveaways for a three-month being, I noticed that on average, the total entrants was about 3,500. Some were far higher, but many (the majority) were well short. You want maximum entrants and a better possibility of winning.

The specifics

I started my first program the day before Thanksgiving. I figured that people would be on vacation and looking at free deals. Second, I ended on the last day of the month, so I had a full week. Also, I chose one book in each category, non-fiction biography, then two types of fiction, action adventure and women's contemporary fiction.

Table 17. Goodreads giveaway results

Details	Chambers	In a Moment	Sue Kim
Length of promo	7 days	7 days	3 months
Final # of entrants	724	517	237 (after 7 days)
Shelved as **Want to Read**	270	211	Not available
Book sales increase	6%	9%	4.5%
Print cost	$30.65	$39.10	$32.75

Two other data points that showed up on my dashboard during this seven-day period:

Added by Unique users: 483

Total books added to shelf: 677

While I posted the giveaway link on my Facebook author page, I completely forgot to do the same on YouTube, Instagram, my blog and on my own Goodreads pages. Five hours prior to the end of the giveaway, I posted a picture on Instagram. The results indicate the numbers would have been much higher if I'd remembered to do these simple acts sooner. But still, for a first time, highly amateur effort, it was worth the effort to get the data.

How do I know that? A marketer will use a simple equation to look at the cost per impression. Using the total investment of the print costs, and estimating the shipping at $5.00 per book, I have a total cost that looks like this:

Program Financials	
Printing costs:	$102.50
Est. shipping ($5/book, 15 people):	$ 75.00
Total investment:	$177.50
Breakdown of cost per result	
Total cost per unique user:	$ .36
Total cost per books placed on shelf:	$ .26

This doesn't include the hundreds (thousands?) of views that the giveaway attracted. If you consider these figures, and compare the dollars spent and actual outcome with the $2,500 I spent on Facebook, you start to get an idea of the differences between a marketing program and a true sales program.

Question 119: When do I use book discounts, and should discounts run concurrently with other promotions?

About the same time I was setting up the schedule for the above promotions, I thought: what the heck, I'll go ahead and try a discount and see what happens. Now, you are probably laughing at me for being so out of touch or reluctant to try a discount, but honestly, after the money that I'd spent on Facebook and then the failed $500 giveaway, (which I thought would go viral and result in sales far in excess of the $500) you can imagine my skepticism.

I am thrilled to report that the discounting effort paid off. The upfront effort was miniscule and the revenue was immediate and identifiable to the program.

The program details

For those of you who haven't yet tried a discount, you temporarily reduce the price of your book on one, or many of your distribution channels. Like the give-away, you set the timeframe for the discount, it's promoted through the third-party entity you have chosen, and then you sit back and watch the results.

I chose a different title in the women's fiction category so I could run the program simultaneously and track the results. That meant I needed to choose an eBook, in order to watch the hour-by-hour/day-to-day sales. Also, I elected to go through MyBookCave. If you will recall, this is the organization that rates books. Since my books were rated and approved, I qualified for their eBook discount promotions.

Why MyBookCave? The primary reason was their subscriber base includes opt-in readers (like myself, actually) who have self-identified what types of books they want to read, and what offers, promotions and discounts they want to see. It's a highly-qualified group of potential readers. This seemed far and away superior to a general mass email.

Even so, a few things to note.

➢ **The schedule**

It gets full quick, and seemingly, authors want the premier times.

I suggested a date, but indicated I was flexible.

- **Reviews**

The book you want to offer must have at least twenty reviews. If it doesn't, then the reviews from three other books you've written must equal 15. The point here, is that MyBookCave doesn't want unproven books being pushed to their subscriber base.

- **Pricing/discount offered**

MyBookCave has specific requirements around the price of an eBook. The timeframes and purchasing options are also identified and required. E.g. the price must be in place 24 hours prior to the discount, pricing on Amazon and other retail outlets must be consistent etc.

This is one reason you will have a hard time if your book is free, all the time, everywhere. You can't participate in this program. MyBookCave, and many others, must have a retail price high enough to justify a discounted price. The lone exception to this is a program called book bundles, where the price ranges from 0-.99 cents. You are one of a number of authors in the bundle.

MyBookCave makes it incredibly hard to screw up or forget key elements of the program. Once a book is approved, emails are sent at intervals reminding you what needs to be done. The price reduction reminders come at five days, three days and then twenty-four hours before the discount goes live. The terms and conditions are clearly spelled out, such as sending books out within two weeks of the promotional end, and identifying consequences author's inability to send out books on time (not participating in future promotions).

Maximizing the effort

Once your book is approved, the announcement will go out to the consumer base of MyBookCave. However, the author/publisher, can select to pay a small fee to customize the target audience in certain genres. This ranges from $20-$25.00, and the lists are in the 20-35,000 range. After looking through the genre lists, I selected the romance category and paid the $20.00 required. I wanted to be sure the discount announcement went to my ideal reader.

Table 18. Book discount results

	Books sold	Royalty at 35% of 1.99
First hour	8 units	.69 X 8 = $5.52
First 23 hours	39 units	.69 x 39 = $26.91
Days 2-4	96 units	.69 x 96 = $66.24
Final day	41 units	.69 x 41 = $28.29
Total sales	**184 units**	**$126.96**

One important data point that's not included in the above is the number of print book sales I realized from this effort. The numbers ranged about 20 per say above average sales, and the royalties on that book are in the range of $2.90. I believe that was probably another $50 dollars, give or take, due to this program.

Total author investment: $20.00 Return: $176.96

Question 119: What if I offend the reader?

Offending these days is pretty darn hard. Firstly, you have a lot of sites that use the rating system to help readers know what they are getting. Organizations like My Book Ratings, which isn't affiliated with any religious or other organization, know what they are doing and the readers know what they are buying. Secondly, many web sites take ratings a step further and add sections for the author to clearly articulate what's in the book (in terms of sex, language, violence etc.).

Perhaps a better question is this: If you've had great editing and super marketing and aren't selling books, then it won't matter if you change your genre or subject because you have no fans to please…except yourself.

Question 120: What's a true sign of a happy reader, and does this translate to sales?

Happy readers are those who refer your books to other readers and come back to buy more. They are also the ones who bring your books to book clubs and debate whether or not you are going to write a sequel. They are also the ones who will show up at a book signing.

Referrals turn into sales, and this is the ultimate evidence of happy, satisfied readers.

Let's look at the story of Amanda Hocking. If you are unfamiliar with the paranormal genre or Hocking's story, it's worth learning. Her story was heralded for the dramatic rise then perceived fall. Industry luminaries blamed it on the unhappiness of readers when she went with a mainstream publisher who immediately raised the prices of her novellas, thereby breaking the trust that she had created with her readers.

> I prefer the word 'satisfied' because it's deeper and longer-lasting and implies a sense of trust between the reader and the author. I hope that I satisfy my readers at a core level

The short version is that Amanda was a physical therapist by day who wrote paranormal books by night. After receiving countless rejections from publishers, she released her entire library (of nine at the time) available only as eBooks. Her pricing strategy was wise: she sold the first book in her trilogy for $.99 cents and raised the sequels to $2.99 each. Her means of creating awareness and marketing was to provide free, eBook copies to reviewers and bloggers. Many wrote great reviews, which encouraged even more awareness, lifting sales further.

In ten months, she sold 1.5 million books (she said about 9,000 per day) and made $2.5 million dollars, the first self-published author in the world to do so.

Her success caught the attention of St. Martin's Press and she signed a $2.1 million-dollar deal. The entire industry was watching as St. Martin's promptly raised the price for her books to $4.99 and up. Sales immediately stalled, then dropped dramatically.

The industry learned that the price point a consumer would pay for a 200-page book sub-three-dollars, but not a penny higher. As the sales plummeted, reader rage followed, and the "Hocking deal" has never been replicated. Now, when publishers evaluate the sales of a 'eBook only' author, they give a hard look at the price points, the length of the novel, the reader base and the pricing elasticity. While Hocking re-signed with St. Martin's Press in 2015, the terms of her deal were not announced.

Question 121: What happens when sales get high enough to attract a tier-three publisher, like an eBook only publisher? Should I consider it?

Once again, it depends on your situation, preferences and what you want to achieve. Let me tell you about my experience.

One day, Peter surprised me with the news that he'd had an offer for *A Convenient Date* from an eBook only publisher. On one hand, I was gratified. The eBook category of publishing is considered to be almost on par with mainstream publishers in the traditional sense of the word. The $5,000 advance was "decent" according to Peter, and the terms were flexible. I could still go ahead and publish with another print-only entity. Furthermore, I'd keep the rights for audio, visual and other forms of media. This is really generous, considering that many romance authors who have existing deals with mainstream publishers are now getting on average a $5,000 advance.

Still, I wasn't sold on the agreement. eBooks are quite profitable, as you can see from the data I have shared, and with very little up-front costs, it doesn't take many sales to recoup the investment. The only value I could see the eBook publisher bringing to the table was ease of process and marketing. As I told Peter, I was now familiar with the process, pricing, design, layout and marketing myself, and wasn't depending on the advances to make a living. Also, by this time, I had established a brand.

As Peter and I explored the notion of self-publishing, POD, and advances, I decided to start my own imprint for women's contemporary fiction. My non-fiction and action-adventure could continue to go mainstream, and if I received that was compelling, I could reissue through another publishing entity.

But the bottom line for me was (and still is) the money. Why give 70% of the profits to the publisher when I could keep it myself? Hocking got $2.5 million dollars-worth of value after initially getting rejected, which is the ultimate answer for ALL aspiring writers.

Peter, to his credit, encouraged me to ignore the offer. As much as he'd like the money from the publishing deal, 15% is small in the grand scheme of the business efforts, and he ultimately knew that this was the best course for me, at least initially.

That's not to say I won't at some point take one or more of my books and put them through traditional channels, but must be the right deal, with the best terms.

Question 122: How do publishers assess the manuscripts provided by agents? In other words, does a ranking system exist?

As one acquisition editor at a major house in New York told me, most editors who receive manuscripts have three piles.

"The pile closest to my desk is for my tier A agents," the editor explained. "They're the ones who consistently bring me manuscripts that turn into bestsellers. The next pile over is the B agents. They are hit and miss," she continued. "Sometime a bestseller and sometimes not. The last pile is the C agents. They are unlikely to have a winner, but their agency has a good track record over all and I don't want to miss anything."

"What about all the other agents that don't have a track record at all?" I asked.

"That's my far pile." She confided to me that she lets her assistant read those at her leisure and says that sometimes she'll find a jewel. "That's what happened with Stephenie Meyer, you know. An editor's assistant picked it up and read it on a plane and the rest is history."

So that's another bit of trivia for you. Despite all the pap that a publishing house will immediately throw away a non-represented manuscript (e.g. it wasn't submitted through a known agent), the odd manuscript will get picked up and read. If it's your time, it's your time.

Question 123: Why are more and more authors creating their own imprint?

Money and control.

Brandilyn Collins published dozens of books with Harper Collins and won a number of awards from the industry, yet she started making plans to leave her publisher five years ago.

"More money in it," she said simply. She'd spent years creating her brand and had a following that trusts her content. It's like a relationship with a hair dresser: you know the hairdresser is going to give you a good cut no matter the salon where he or she works.

Question 124: Is it hard to create your own imprint?

Not hard, but it is time consuming and it's critical that you are a detail person. On top of that, a few peculiarities exist regarding the issuance of ISBN numbers. ISBNs are free if you allow CreateSpace or Nook to be identified as the publisher. This is a dead giveaway you have self-published the book.

Another downside (as I learned) of having CreateSpace or Nook issue the ISBN is that this can be a detriment to changes later on. For example, after I created my own imprint, I wanted to make changes/remove and combine my titles. I didn't have the flexibility to do what I wanted because I hadn't purchased the original ISBNs. If you want to establish your own imprint in the market, you, acting as the publisher, must purchase the ISBN's directly from Bowker and register the book, format, and all associated details with the edition you are listing. Only then will your imprint name be listed when you choose to publish with one of the POD services. Its more money upfront, but worth it in the long run if you believe you will continue writing and build a library of books under one imprint name.

Question 125: But I only have one book. Is it worth it?

Oh, how I wish someone had given me the perspective years ago that I'm now going to share with you.

Think long-term. If you are a one-book or one-idea only author and have a passion project that you just need to get out of you, then no, absolutely not. Go with either CreateSpace, Nook or any other group and call it a day. However, if this is just the start of your career and you envision more than four or five books, which I think is the tipping point, then yes, you create your own imprint.

Also, I can cite many authors who start out publishing their own works and then go on to publish other aspiring authors who don't have the time (or money) to work with an independent publisher or do it on their own.

This year alone, I've been approached by three aspiring authors to publish their books. One of the three made my personal cut for quality, but in that case, it was so good, I introduced him to my agent, and I truly think he has a shot at a major deal. I would be doing him a great disservice to publish his book under my imprint, even though the selfish side of me was tempted to keep him to myself!

Question 126: Are local bookstores receptive to books by self-published authors?

My experience has been great because I was doing one fundamental thing: I was creating demand for my book through the school system and encouraging/requiring those schools to purchase books through the local bookstore. This resulted in a strong relationship with the bookstore who didn't have to purchase the book upfront, carry the stock or return the unpurchased portions. Schools were coming in purchasing 20-30 books at a time.

You could be a writer of a non-fiction book speaking at local VA Hospitals, retirement homes or church groups and use the exact same approach. Here are a few things to know before approaching the local bookstore:

- Inventory for bookstores are based upon the author's ability to pull through demand from group buyers.
- Author drops off and pick up the books.

- Author pays cost of returns. On this subject, establish the policy on returns before you provide books. You can have a 'no return' policy or a return only if the spine isn't broken etc.
- Author must provide re-stock and inventory.
- Retail expects a 40-60% discount off the list price.
- Retail offers educational clients-group discounts of 20-30%

Many retailers actually like books by self-published authors because the margin is better, although the biggest complaint is the inability for authors to drive demand and maintain high stock numbers.

Author Career Options

CHAPTER HIGHLIGHTS

- *Co-authoring*
- *Events and speaking*
- *Consulting and workshops*

The book is the calling card. The money comes from all the things that surround it.

Sarah Gerdes

Authors have so many opportunities to earn income beyond book royalties, the topic deserves an entire chapter. Had I had an inkling of the benefits of authoring, I would have starting seriously writing a decade sooner than I did. If the previous chapters took a little of the wind form your sails, this chapter will replace that sail with a tsunami. I'll reveal specific amounts I've been paid for alternative author options (how I made money from everything but the book), as well as those of other authors. Most authors I reference in this chapter requested anonymity because in their minds (not mine) it's considered bad form to make more money on non-book revenue. Is it considered shameful, I wonder, that an author accepts money for events or contract jobs? I hope not, because it is just one of the credible, legitimate ways of earning money while you write a novel.

Question 127: How can I make money while I'm writing my own novel?

The following tables lists the job opportunities along with average project fees.

Table 19. Author income opportunities

Job	Description	Money
Author for hire	Contracted by project- your name is on it	Negotiable- $500+
Ghost-writer	Book/other- anonymous	$1-$20,000 for a book
Speaking	Keynote	$500+
Workshops	Teacher/speaker	$250-$750
Schools	Speaker	$250-$750
Editor	Variable	Per project ($50/hr.+)
Company	Hired to speak at internal events or provide services on your book topic	Negotiable- $1,500+

Question 128: What is an author for hire? Is it common?

Contracting an author is very common. Not all private or even publicly-held companies have the luxury of hiring a full-time writer. Furthermore, many independent publishers want a dependable writer for contract-for-hire projects: those that have your name on the title but the publisher owns the copyright.

I know two authors who are excellent writers but willingly admit they have a hard time coming up with original story ideas. One called her plight as being "storyless." She, and the other author, turned to the task of writing other people's stories, non-fiction and fiction alike. It's become a huge market, one which you might not even be aware exists.

The unique aspect of this scenario is that the publishing entity—the organization that comes up with the actual storyline--keeps all the rights associated with the book, and makes deals for other channels (television, movies). The Work for Hire (WFH) agreement states this explicitly. That's doesn't mean you can't financially benefit.

Still unconvinced? Let me give you a personal example. During my slow years, when I was having a hard time writing anything publishers wanted, Peter called me and said he had a proposal. A certain publishing firm had a model that worked well for available (e.g. unemployed) authors: they provided the storyline and the author would write the book. They paid $7,500 per completed manuscript, and the books were about 225 pages.

Interested, and with nothing to lose, I accepted and decided to audition for the job, so to speak. It was like a fashion show for prospective authors. I was given an outline, as were a handful of other prospective authors, and then we were asked to write the first thirty pages. From these samples, the author would be chosen.

Peter was delighted when the publishing firm gave their response: they loved my approach and writing and would be interested in my submission for the next project—as the one I'd written for had gone to an existing writer in their stable.

Between the time I received the next submission opportunity, I'd started writing *Chambers* and I declined to move forward with another submission. Had I accepted, or been chosen for this role, it could have been a revenue stream, at $7,500 per book.

Personal projects

Another common WFH are personal projects, such as family histories, personal biographies and the like. I know a photographer who was asked to catalog a ranching operation. He learned the photographs were part of a larger, multi-generational project. It required the talents of a real author, not a marketing person creating photo captions. He asked around, searched on the Internet for a few writers, placed cold-calls, and eventually two authors were interviewed for the project. The one chosen received $3,000 for about six weeks' worth of work. It's not a full-time job, but the extra income is enough to pay a few bills, afford a getaway or to edit a novel.

Independent author and aspiring novelist Andy Thomas is based in northern Britain. I came to know him through Instagram, a social media platform that is fabulous for authors to use for connecting with readers. Over time, I've learned that he pays the bills by being a marketing and technical writer, and editor for local businesses, but two times in the last year, he took on what I define as personal projects for local individuals. Each one paid about 1,000 pounds and took less than thirty days.

"It's not a lot but every bit helps," he said, referencing his own plans to use the money to edit his first, full-length novel.

Consider your personal situation. Do you have the desire to take on local projects or ones that are outside your comfort zone of authoring? You put the word out proactively or even ask local businesses or families if they are interested in writing a family history or personal biography. If so, this may be an immediate area of new income.

For writing the authorized biography of Sue Kim, I was paid a flat fee of $20,000. I hold copyright on the work, and it's published under my own imprint. The reason for this was purely financial. I split the proceeds with the family who hired me, and I manage all the business aspects, including bearing the costs of the publishing, distribution, marketing and promotion.

Before providing the quote for the price I was going to charge for writing the book, I spoke with a number of ghost writers and contract writers for biographies and learned that $20,000 is a standard fee unless the author has a name for writing nothing but biographies. It's a sub-specialty of writing and didn't apply to me. In hindsight, my fee was lower than it should have been, because I greatly underestimated the amount of work required to complete the project.

I thought it would take me six months to research and interview subjects: it took me nearly two years and multiple trips to complete that phase. Writing was another eighteen months, with drafts, reviews by the family and edits. Do all projects have this type of complexity? Probably not, but this book was worth the effort. It has since been optioned for film and an Off-Broadway play.

Question 129: Why does one become a ghost author?

In the case of Pam Liflander, my first strategic editor, she had a long and successful history in publishing. She was a former acquisitions editor in New York, with several major publishing houses, shepherding many books to the top of the bestseller list. When she left her full-time position to raise her children outside the city, she became a free-lance strategic editor, taking on clients like myself.

Over time I learned that she had been asked by a publisher to step in when a signed author was well behind schedule, or completely failing at the task of writing their manuscript. Pam was asked to re-write sections, then the sections became chapters, and eventually she was asked to overhaul entire books. She was contracted as a ghost writer. Her ability to be the ultimate editor gave her the role of the author. After a few years, Liflander had amassed bestselling books for a variety of authors.

As her reputation grew, so did her clout. She got an agent and asked to be listed as the co-author on the books. More bestselling books followed, and she now has her own career as an author. It's been a nearly twelve-year journey for her, one that was unplanned but natural and fulfilling, mentally and financially.

Question 130: Should I co-author with a friend/acquaintance?

This is a tangential topic to authoring, so I've placed it in this section, but it doesn't usually pay money upfront. If it did, it would be considered a WFH, like the type Pam Liflander did early on. She was listed on the front cover and paid a flat fee.

The question of "should I?" is one that only you can answer. Co-authoring has a few elements that set the situation up for failure, much like going into business with a relative. A few considerations are:

Who will be the primary author? E.g. the one with the ideas, who will establish the flow, the tenor of the book and write the majority of the manuscript.

Will this be a true, co-authoring situation, where the chapters will rotate between the two (or more) co-authors? Some authoring teams choose this route in order to get equal time on the page. The risk is the tenor, tone and even language will conflict. It's challenging for a reader to go back and forth between tones and perspectives. If the book has been sold to a publisher, the managing editor will have the responsibility of smoothing out the rough spots.

Many times, a celebrity or well-known personality is paired with a co-author. That individual is a professional and is able to submerge his or her own ego for the project. Imagine going through this process with a friend. With all the nuances and emotions involved, it is not a setting for success.

This past summer, I observed three individuals—all professionals—who had a shared interest and enthusiasm for a particular non-fiction subject. After listening to their idea, I agreed it had merit and shared my non-fiction proposal template with them. They wrote up a full proposal and submitted it to an agent who sold the project to a publisher.

Then the wheels fell off the dragster.

While they'd thought through the roles of each person (primary author, primary editor, primary researcher) and apportioned the book in 1/3 allotments, they had three different voices, visions, working styles and time availability. The project ended up stalling, then fracturing, then it fell apart completely. They ended up giving back the advance. Fortunately, they still maintain a relationship with one another, but are not as close as they once were.

If you are considering co-authoring a book, here's a checklist:

- Philosophically, do we have the same vision for the book? E.g. the content, direction, tone and theme.
- How will we collaborate and resolve our differences of opinion?
- How will services be paid (editing, marketing etc.)?
- How we maintain tone throughout is to have a primary author. Who will fill that role?
- If non-fiction, who will conduct the research, check the facts and interview the subject if necessary?
- How will we split up promotional duties/obligations?

Question 131: What does speaking at events really mean?

Let's tackle the first part by clarifying a speaker versus a keynote speaker, a moderator or a panelist.

- **Keynote**

You are hired to give the major speech/presentation of the event. It is typically 30-40 minutes, and it's up to the organization to provide compensation. Some do, others don't, but if you are going to be flown in for the keynote, all travel and expense costs are covered by the entity. You receive top billing in all materials. The lead time ranges from 6-9 months depending on the nature and size of the event.

- **Speaker, moderator or panelist**

If you are starting out, you aren't going to get a keynote position right out of the gate. You will work your way up from being a panelist, then a moderator, speaker and finally keynote. When in these roles, you typically won't receive monetary compensation, but your name will be listed in all the marketing and promotional material.

This has tremendous value. Young professionals in any industry gain credibility, recognition, referrals and clients through the exposure of participating on panels. It's a necessary step towards the goal of one day being a paid speaker.

➢ **Private institutions**

This can be a church, a private school, or any other entity who thinks that you and your story are interesting. Hands down, corporate events are the most lucrative. Different departments have off-site or in-house forums where special guests are invited to speak. These always have budgets attached—always. Travel and expenses are paid and usually a day-rate per diem is provided.

About four months ago, I was contacted by a health and wellness company to speak at their annual retreat. It's a small company, with eight full-time employees and revenues of $1.5M per year. They didn't have a budget for a speaker, but the event was held at a lakeside resort about an hour from my home, so I was made an offer. In return for speaking at a dinner the first evening and moderating a session the following morning, I'd receive an all-expense paid series of spa treatments for a half day. The cost of travel, meals and lodging would also be included.

Between the cost of the resort, food and spa treatment prices, the value was around $900. In truth, I was happier to have a break at a resort and a spa treatment instead of the cash, because I would have used the money for something practical and not treating myself to a half-day of bliss.

Question 132: I'm just an aspiring author. How could I possibly get started in speaking and then get paid?

I'm going to pick on two aspiring novelists I've mentioned earlier, Andy and Rachel. Both have interesting backgrounds that would appeal to different audiences. Some of my ideas for them include a few which have worked for me.

Andy's pitch: military background, one that entails jumping out of planes. He has faced danger and death, ultimately ending his career in an elite squad. He's endured hardship and loss, personal sacrifices and yet faces life in an optimistic way, both professionally and personally. Who should he approach about being a speaker and how would his contribution help the group?

- **Schools: Career Days**

Career days are common in the US and abroad, generally for juniors and seniors. Andy can talk about the benefits of the military but also about writing as a profession, for clients and for himself. Pay for career day: nothing.

I've been involved in more than a half a dozen high school career days and I truly enjoyed each event. The students sign up for 5 different sessions during the day, each one lasting roughly 45 minutes. Other contributors include dozens of professionals from physicians, to attorneys, elected officials—you name it. Outside the fun of answering questions from the students and teachers alike (have you ever met Tom Cruise? How much money do you really make?), the networking with the other speakers is always beneficial.

This effort has led to other opportunities at the high school level, which are included in the section below.

➢ **Events at schools**

Here in the US, most schools have PTA funds that are used for visiting authors, and this can be allocated in any capacity deemed beneficial. For instance, it can be used for workshops, symposiums or speaking, but I want to emphasize the money is secondary to the effort, and this is the mindset you should have when talking with schools. The first goal is to get enlighten, educate and to some degree, entertain the students.

With the subject matter of Andy's works, elementary school is out, but not junior high or high school. For these schools, I'd recommend a different take. There he could do a writing workshop and because of his background in both technical and marketing writing, he could go in with the pitch to the English teacher (or librarian) about a two or three-part series of writing development.

Now, older readers may think this is absurd. Why would a junior high or high school student need or want to learn how to do about writing development? One word: money.

Blogs bring in a lot of advertising revenue, the more followers the higher the payout. Further, the social media explosion has given people of all ages an audience. Advertisers pay to get at this audience. The better the voice of the individual posting the blog, Instagram, Facebook or other social media snippet the more money is to be made. Young adult (teens) can work at McDonald's or write from home. Give them a choice.

➢ Author Pay: starting at $150 on up. A few examples to share with you. I was asked do a reading of Chambers. I was contacted by the school librarian, who informed me the budget for the year was already spent but was hoping I would come in anyway. I did it for free, and was glad I did. I was next contacted by an English teacher who asked if I'd come for two sessions with her class to talk about the writing process. She was going to purchase 30 copies of my book and use it as an example of writing technique. She had no budget for my time but had purchased the books (educational institutions receive a 60% discount for books). I agreed and the following month I spent two hours with her and the class, and then probably another two hours reading their summary reports.

The following spring, she contacted me again, requesting my time for a three-session workshop with her students for the following year. This time, she had a budget of $450 total. I put it on my calendar and agreed. I did, however, request that $150 of that be spent on books for her library and I kept the rest. Good will and giving back go hand-in-hand. Every year from that time until I moved states, I returned to her school and provided that workshop to her students.

One other engagement comes to mind. The librarian of an elementary school contacted me about reading to a group of students. The fee of $750 was significant and I accepted. While I was thrilled to walk into an auditorium full of 800 students, from first to sixth grade, that emotion changed to dismay when I learned that many of the students came from immigrant families and knew little English—but were a mix of twelve languages!

I will honestly say that I don't believe half of the children understood a word I was saying, and because I'd not asked enough questions before hand (having never encountered this before) my presentation was not as entertaining to the students as I thought it should be. Afterward, I asked the librarian to keep the money and to invest it in books for the library. She was delighted. Unbeknownst to me, she pitched me to speak at the Washington State convention for librarians, the mother-of-all events for librarians in the state. It was an amazing opportunity, which would have made a big impact on my careers and sales. Sadly, it never came to pass. The day I was to speak, I gave birth to my first daughter. Still, you can see by example the benefits of giving your time and effort to the local school system.

- **Local corporations or associations**

Both private and non-profit groups have money, and even the associations that claim to have zero budget for visiting speakers are an untapped goldmine. The associations are comprised of members who are—you guessed it—employed at privately held companies who do have funds.

For Andy, I would modify the pitch that was made to the schools for these groups, adapted to their unique market or interest area. Intense background, lots of challenges, overcoming the odds, succeeding, motivating and skill development. Added to this is pursuing the dream while you are paying the bills.

Every individual, corporation or non-profit group, entrepreneur or worker-bee, wants to know how to keep hope alive and stay focused in times of turmoil. This is his essential pitch as a person and an author. The pay for this? It might initially be free, but the fees for a speaker can start at $250 and range up to $1,250. Once you have a name brand established and a series of events under your belt, this can be much higher. More on this in the marketing and sales section.

- **Book clubs- on line/virtual**

These are forums that shouldn't be overlooked. On-line or virtual books clubs mean that the group may or may not meet in person (usually they do), but the author calls in for the discussion. It's a fun way to interact directly with readers.

- Author Pay: zero. Just a lot of reader love, which is priceless.

Rachel Parker's pitch: a young woman with many physical disabilities who must constantly overcome daily challenges but who serves as an inspiration to those who know her. Endowed with a sense of humor, humility and diversity, she can speak to others who need to be motivated and encouraged to get more out of life.

- **Local non-profits**

Specifically, St. Vincent's and the Salvation Army, to cite well-known regional and national organizations. Local shelters for domestic abuse and other groups who help lift those in need to a better place in life. The local Rotary, while a business entity, serves this community on a regular basis.

Rachel could speak on courage, discipline, overcoming fears, facing and overcoming the judgement of others. She is well positioned to talk about boosting your confidence and the power of focus, because she literally started from nothing to get to where she is today. Is her work published? No, but it will be independently published in 2018, and at that point she can use it as a calling card. The pay: nothing up to a modest $150. The exception to this is when a fundraiser is being held, a well-known executive or celebrity is brought in, but the funds for this are taken out of the sponsorship money.

Rachel also has a few opportunities to speak at schools. The uplifting, motivational message of persevering is a strong and compelling one. As her library of books grows, she could contribute to the educational institutions to a broader degree.

- **Women's groups**

Most areas, even my rather small city of 28,000, have dozens of groups for women, from farming, to food, to knitting. Most of the organizations have causes they support (kids, cancer, domestic abuse, pet shelters). Rachel could approach groups that support a cause she is passionate about and provide her time and talents by being a speaker to the organization. Groups always welcome a fresh face with an uplifting message. The outcome? Almost always book sales, but just as important for the long term, relationships that last.

Question 133: Could I become and editor or proofreader?

Certainly, if you have the skills to do so, but beware. The trap of becoming a freelance editor is that becomes a full-time job as opposed to spot income like speaking at an event, holding a workshop or giving a motivational talk. Editorial work, especially if you are good, will expand until it consumes all your time. Proofing is a nice side job, and is less time consuming than editing, however you are going to have the challenge of success without the monetary benefits, as it pays significantly less than editing or speaking events. However, it can be more consistent, so you must analyze the tradeoffs.

Question 134: How do I break into speaking at corporate events?

You start by put speaking information on your website identifying you are available to speak. This will likely result in invitations at local events where you will gain exposure to the business community. You may also want to consider being represented by a local speaker bureau, although I must plug Speakermatch.com, where you can post your information for free, identify and select potential speaking opportunities and connect directly.

Given what you have read about individual book sales in Chapter Nine, and the small dollar amounts, you can see why and how so many author's turn to events and other activities to increase income.

I'll give you an example. Most metropolitan areas have entrepreneur groups such as Entrepreneur Organization (formally called The Young Entrepreneur Organization, or YEO). I was asked to speak at a local gathering of the YEO of a hundred CEO's (under the age of 30) of companies with more than a million dollars in revenue, located in Seattle, WA. This was offered to me without compensation. Following this, I was invited to speak at the regional YEO event with hundreds of CEOs from a tri-state area. I was compensated $1,250 for the keynote.

In another instance, I was invited to the *Inc. Magazine's* Annual 500 gathering. I'd been featured in the publication and even wrote guest editorials. For this event, I was asked to give a keynote for one of the evenings, but also offer individual sessions to the attendees, in groups of about 100-300, depending on who attended the session. Beyond that, I moderated a roundtable and led several other exercises. Total compensation: $3,000, not including the travel and accommodations which were covered. They had a $5,000 budget for my entire package, and that's probably what it came down to.

The primary message is that the book is the evidence of your knowledge, and this pays dividends. Before *Navigating the Partnership Maze* was published, my total speaking fees amounted to $0.00. I'd been speaking for over ten years at all sorts of technology industry forums, women's events, entrepreneur symposiums, and even for business publications, but I never received a dollar for my efforts.

> Don't be surprised if you make far more money from speaking than you do from books. It's not unlike the music industry, where concerts provide far more income for the artist than sales of songs.

Somehow, someway, having a book "legitimized" my knowledge. Within six months of the book's release, I'd earned over $20,000 in speaking fees alone (the income from corporate projects was separate).

Question 135: How does a book impact corporate projects?

Corporate projects typically result from non-fiction, how-to titles. I have a favorite story that illustrates the power of a non-fiction book.

After I started my own business, I'd been working with Microsoft for years, creating partnerships and revenue producing agreements on behalf of clients. The value of the deals were in the millions of dollars, but try as I might, I couldn't cajole, convince or win Microsoft as a client, even when I wasn't representing competitive firms.

One month after my book on partnerships was published, I spoke at a local Women Entrepreneur's Forum (EWF), which I'd set up a few months prior in anticipation of the book release. Among the thirty or so women in attendance (they paid $30 each to attend, while I was speaking for free), was one man. Prior to the talk, we had technical difficulties. He willingly came up and fixed the problems, making some comment about how Microsoft software was always having issues.

After the thirty minute talk was over, I answered questions, the group dispersed and the man stayed behind. He gave me his card and asked me to call him. Turns out he led a product group at Microsoft and he needed partner-related guidance, which was why he'd attended the presentation.

Two weeks later, I'd signed Microsoft as a client, and the fee for the first, two-week project was $10,000. Following that was another project for $20,000. When another division learned about my work, I was hired and the ball was officially rolling because I became an authorized vendor, a coveted status. That year alone, I made nearly $80,000 from Microsoft as a client, more than I'd made from the book royalties to that time. It was the book that opened other doors that were previously closed, and is one of the reasons why professionals write how-to books. The book is a loss leader for the corporate, client work that follows afterward.

I began to look at the book as an investment as opposed to the reward. You may wonder why I moved into fiction, which is a much less lucrative adventure (for me), wherein I was essentially started over at the very bottom of the food chain. The reason is because I, too, had a dream to pursue, one where passion outweighed the money, and still does.

Ownership, Rights & Estate Planning

CHAPTER HIGHLIGHTS

- *Ideas & infringement*
- *Copyrights*
- *Attorneys*

The right to be attributed as an author of a work is not merely a copyright, it is every author's basic human right
Kalyan C. Kankanala

Having copyright paperwork is never critical until someone steals your work and passes it off as their own, on YouTube, in front of tens of thousands of viewers. That's what happened to me, and it was a violation in the truest sense of the word. Worse, the individual who had stolen the material (it's a harsh word but truly deserved) had done such a fantastic job of marketing the video, it received thousands more views than my own, giving him lots of advertising revenue and me lots of stomach pains.

This chapter takes you through the essentials of copyright. It's just one of the legalities you need to be thinking about as you write your novel. Other aspects, such as your estate and potential situations should also be thought about now, not later. I've been to a few legal rodeos and while I've gotten bruised, the effects haven't left scars, and for that, I'm grateful.

The number one message is to anticipate every event which may take place, no matter how outlandish it may seem. You never know. It could happen to you.

Question 136: What are the rights of the author, and what is a copyright?

You, the creator of a work (all contracts typically refer to the manuscript as "the work"), are the rightful owner. You copyright this work with a central organization in order to protect yourself against unlawful use of your work--theft of the content, in the form of plagiarism, to be specific.

When you decide to bring the work to market through another entity, then you assign the rights to publish that work to that third-party. That entity could be any person or organization, and the specific type of publishing is defined within the contract details. You could give one entity the eBook rights (which some people do) and the rights to a Broadway musical to another entity, then you could give the movie rights to yet another, and so on.

Typically, a first-time author who is signed by a mainstream publisher ends up signing away all rights. This isn't out of stupidity; it's smart business on the part of the publisher. That publisher is taking all the risk and absorbing all the editing, marketing, production, distribution and sales costs. That has a value, and it's in the thousands. For the investment in the author, the publisher (again, typically the print publisher) wants to maximize the return on investment. The first-time author is usually very happy to sign on the dotted line (myself included). It's only years later, when the royalty checks take so long and the other avenues of revenue aren't being fully explored does the author regret the contract.

Question 137: What do I need to do for copyrighting my work?

If your book is under contract with a publisher, that organization will automatically complete the registration on your behalf.

According to the U.S. copyright, your unpublished work is already under copyright protection, which "... protects an author's expression in literary, artistic, or musical form." U.S. Copyright suggests that you put a copyright notice on all unpublished copies of your work. This puts readers on notice that it is your copyrighted material.

To register:

You can do this on-line by at the U.S. Electronic Copyright offices. The website is https://copyright.gov/registration/. One tip: at first glance it looks like your cost will be a few hundred dollars. Read the fine print. The average cost to copyright your book should be closer to about $55.00.

Question 138: How do I get my rights back?

When phrased liked this, it's referring to the publishing rights. That means you, the copyright holder or the creator and owner of the information, have given the rights to publish your work to another entity.

To get your rights back, you, the author, must request the rights back from the publisher. Sometimes this is completed through an on-line form, and other times, it must be done in writing, the request sent to the rights and copyright deparment.

Question 139: When, then, does getting your rights back come in to play?

When your book has stopped selling for a long period (as in years) or you believe the publisher isn't marketing your book and/or you could do a better job. Another reason is that you want to create a second edition, or build a series on a title, but are prevented from doing this due to the contractual terms.

Why, you will ask, if a book has stopped selling, won't the publisher give the rights back to the author? It's because publishers aren't in the business of proactively looking up your sales figures and offering to give an author back the rights to a book. An author must ask for their rights to be returned.

Why publishers aren't incentivized to return rights

- **Potential opportunity**

What if your next book (the one you self-published) does really well? It might lift the sales of earlier releases.

- **Good press**

You might be highly profiled, raising the sales of all the books in your library.

- **Alternative offer**

Your book might be picked up for a made-for-tv show, movie or even a podcast series. The publisher assigns certain rights to that entity and make a percentage off your product.

Question 140: Do any guidelines for getting rights back exist?

- Books that have not sold well for over 5 years are likelier to have rights reverted back to the author.
- Typical timeframe is 18 months for the rights to be returned.
- Larger publishers use the DocuSign application for on-line signature. A follow-up email comes about a week later, reconfirming the rights return.
- The moment you receive this document, you are free to take

100% of the content and have it retyped/reformatted.

- You will need to create a new cover. That is usually the property of the publisher who paid for it, assuming the illustrator was in-house. If not, the copyright owner (the illustrator) can be contacted if you want to re-use it the cover.

Process to getting your rights back

1. Write a letter or submit on-line, if your publisher has a form.
2. Identify that you want a return of rights and fill in the commentary/request area. Most require you put in a reason for rights return.
3. Follow-up and wait.
4. Upon receipt of the rights document, file it away.

Many authors who have requested and received the rights returned to them have chosen the course I did with McGraw-Hill. I chose to create new cover art, use my own imprint and match the look and feel of the other books in my library. This entails having new ISBN's assigned and starting from scratch with the book production process.

Question 141: Why wouldn't a publisher use every available avenue of revenue for a book?

Opportunity cost. For instance, with my bestselling trade book, *Navigating the Partnership Maze* (NTPM) it could have been in an audio form of any type, podcasts, you name it. But McGraw-Hill wasn't going to spend the time or money, and I was forbidden to do it myself. I had the desire and the money to do so, but was turned down every time I asked. It was unbelievably frustrating.

A personal story

NTPM was on the shelves for nearly 18 years, an unheard-of number in the non-fiction world. Even now, I have people asking for an updated version, but I didn't want to sign another contract with MH that would lock me out of all my rights again. So, I decided to wait it out. Good thing I'm patient, because two decades is a looong time to wait.

Typically, a publishing house won't issue a paperback if the hardcover is still selling. It's simple economics. The higher price point, the greater the profit. Alternately, the book is selling just enough that the publisher doesn't want to rock the boat and spend more money that they won't make back in the end.

Well, during the last two weeks of writing this manuscript, I woke up one day and received the DocuSign paperwork for the return of rights for NTPM. I'd started three years earlier. Now that I have the rights, I'll create an updated edition and parlay the content into video snippets, podcasts and an audio version of the book.

One other note is that McGraw-Hill identified why they elected not to create a paperback. It was in fact, because the hardcover version presented such higher margins. As I look to the future of this title, I will update the content, and make it available in three formats: paperback, hardcover and hardcover with a flap. The reader has a choice, and I have different profit margins.

Question 142: I've been told I can't copyright a title. Is that true?

Yes. The U.S. Copyright Office explicitly states that titles are not considered intellectual property and therefore can't be copyrighted. The Office defines titles as "short slogans" which are not eligible for copyright protection. That said, you CAN copyright a *title series.* I learned this when I came up with the title for my NTPM. I used *Partnership for Dummies* as a starting point. My agent, Matt Wagner, coughed and told me no.

"You can't use *Dummie* in the title because it's copyrighted." He then told me about the law and I felt a little silly. Matt was the agent who represented the Dummie authors, so he knew better than anyone!

He then suggested I use the online search in the U.S. Copyright Office, which I did, and eventually came up with a new title.

Question 143: What's a typical example of copyright infringement?

Excerpts of your work being taken, reused and not sourced. In the non-fiction world, pulling a quote, paragraph or excerpt is common. The key is to source that usage.

From the four non-fiction books I've written (this is the fifth), I've had dozens of instances where my work has been lifted and not sourced. About twice a year, I go on a tear and spend about a week using key words from each of my books and seeing what comes up in a search. Since the nomenclature I use in my books is unique to me, and written in my style/content, it's relatively easy to find.

When the lifting is minor, I let it go. But if it's more than a sentence or two, I'll send off a note to the author, editor or publisher and suggest that the sentences are similar/identical and that my work must be sourced or the language changed. I almost always get a response within forty-eight hours, and the referenced material is either removed or assigned to me as the source.

I've found that the proactive, soft-touch is better than the hammer. Specifically, I suggest it might be an oversight rather than intentional.

Excerpts taken, reused and repurposed for profit

With the Sue Kim book, I've had copyright infringement both in print as well as video. My book was printed in the US, not South Korea, and yet copies of my book have appeared in bookstores in that country and I can't do a thing about it. Why? South Korea's intellectual property and copyright laws are almost non-existent. My lawyers have told me I could spend a fortune and the government is unlikely to enforce the copyright. Only the major companies such as Samsung, Apple or a motion picture studio has any chance of winning a copyright lawsuit, and even then, it costs millions.

So, what did I do? I grind my teeth and let it go. My only consolation is that whoever is behind the unauthorized publishing and distribution is using the book in full, along with my name.

I've already related the incident about YouTube, but I'll give you the epilogue. When a video is taken down due to copyright infringement, a noticed is posted on the offenders site, which says the video was in copyright violation. The rightful owner of the copyright is listed, the URL as well as the email address (so now one of my emails is listed for the world to see). Those redirects now go to my site, which is a silver lining.

Question 144: What do I when my video has been infringed upon?

A LOT of authors are reading their books and putting the videos up on YouTube. If a third-party is taking excerpts (even two seconds count as infringement), then you need to fill out a copyright complaint. YouTube has a formal process, which includes you identifying the original content source (your URL), the infringing parties site (their URL), the time stamps that explicitly show when the infringement starts, and other details required for the YouTube legal group to review and consider.

Estate planning

Question 145: How do I protect myself in the event of a divorce, death or bankruptcy?

Although I'm not a lawyer, I've had plenty of advice on this subject and paid lots of money over the last twenty years to learn about this topic. Part of the answer depends on your philosophy about marriage/partnerships, and then also how much you are willing to pay to protect yourself against the unknown.

Divorce

Royalties are treated like any other asset; it needs to get divided and a decision will be made to either buy out the other party for a one-time fee, or that other party will receive a share of the royalties for a period of time (or all eternity!). I know one author ended up buying out their partner for a flat-fee of $300,000. Obviously, the author was making a lot of money, however, the marriage lasted for nearly twenty-years and the partner had materially helped in the work, such as editing and marketing the books.

Splitting royalties has become common. Specifically, one party receives the eBook royalties while the other receives royalties from the print book(s). All sorts of things are possible.

You can prevent disputes by using a pre-nuptial agreement, or a post-nuptial agreement.

Death, Estate and bankruptcy

When you are considering legal documents, separate the discussion into two areas: who holds the copyright and who receives the incoming royalties. Most of the time, the lawyers focus on the recipient of the money: your immediate family, extended relatives, or friend. That's the easy part. The copyright holder is the really big decision. It's that person who can determine to continue writing under your name once you are deceased or to turn your classic novel into a cartoon. Unless you proactively determine who will hold the copyright to your works upon your death, then it will be up to the heirs to fight it out or the court to divvy up the ownership.

Your legacy

If you wish to maintain the spirit of your work, you need to use the power of the law. Put into writing the specific Do's and Do nots for your work. Book by book, your desires must be detailed. The executor of the estate (I recommend two executors who serve as a check and balance to one another) is responsible for ensuring your will is executed.

Bankruptcy or Worse

Without exploring all the types of bankruptcy that can actually be filed, the easiest and most cost-effective way to protect your work from being part of a bankruptcy filing is to put the copyright in a trust. This trust then becomes the holder of the copyright. Royalties are made to the name of the trust (instead of Sarah Gerdes it goes to Trust ABC). The trust, in turn, cuts check to whomever it wants, on whatever schedule it wants. It is therefore protected from seizure, not just from bankruptcy but also a lawsuit. Think of being involved in a bad accident where you are personally sued. Having your assets in a trust protects this income from being touched.

Source to read

A wonderful article on rights, copyrights and termination of the rights of heirs is at http://copylaw.com/new_articles/copyterm.html. It gives a thorough description of many scenarios that are invaluable to an author.

Questions for Sarah

CHAPTER HIGHLIGHTS

- *Getting personal*
- *Favorites*
- *Final tips and tidbits*

Hope is not a strategy.

(one of my favorite quotes from years ago in business)

This chapter is comprised of questions people typically only ask when they are drunk, know me really well or submit anonymously. In other words, the fun ones, the serious ones and those that are deeply personal.

Question 146: What is the best process for editing a book?

To be clear, when I hear this question and the word "edit," I'm thinking of strategic editing, such as characters, narrative flow, etc. Through trial and error, I've found my head to be the clearest when I set a book down for a week, work on another project (or no project at all) and come back to it. Second, when I do, I try and read for pleasure, not to "edit" per se. Lastly, I almost always 'edit' while I'm in the bathtub or on the treadmill, and on my Kindle. The common thread, besides sweating, is total dedication to what I'm looking at with zero interruptions from my family, my cell phone or the computer. Nothing disturbs me and that also lends to my heightened concentration level.

> When I'm reading for pleasure, and in that frame of mind, I see things that don't appear when I'm in the original creative mode.

Question 147: What's your best process for catching errors?

When I receive the proof copies back (or the last print out from a mainstream publisher), I read that hard copy. It's really the only way I find errors at all.

Question 148: Do you have favorite tools or habits that you use when you write?

Like a baseball player has his superstitions, I guess I do have a few favorite items that have one thing in common: they all make me happy when I use them.

- I go to my happy place (in the morning, it's looking towards the lake, in the evening, on the couch in front of the fireplace).
- When writing the first outlines of a new book, I use a pen I had custom made for me that's heavy yet smooth. It is substantial and makes me feel like my work is important.

Question 149: Why did you start writing?

The non-fiction books had to do with my earlier career in business. The best thing to come out of that was the knowledge I could start and finish a book. Had I not been obligated to a contract, I'm not sure I'd ever have done it on my own.

Fiction writing first started because I was on bedrest and was looking for more to read. But my dedication and interest continued after I went through the hardships I described earlier in the book and wanted uplifting, hope-filled books that left me feeling good about myself and others.

Question 150: What's the coolest place writing has taken you?

Switzerland, through the Alps and down into Italy, to and through the Lake Cuomo area, Milan and back again. I'd not thought of it before my first women's fiction, but most of my international travel prior to writing had been business-related. Once I turned on the creative side of my writing, the world seemed to figuratively open up and I experience travel differently. It created a desire incorporate ideas, cultures, people and situations into my writing. According to my editor and agent, traveling unexpectedly (but happily) rounded out my ability to create scenes and provide a richer experience for myself as the author, but also, given the reviews and feedback, for the reader as well.

Question 151: How many books do you read on a monthly basis?

No more than one every two weeks. I simply don't have the time, and honestly, I feel guilty taking away time from my own writing. Unless a book completely absorbs me, my mind will wander back to my latest project and I'll get distracted. This leads to a feeling of guilt and I'll put the book down, never to return to it.

Question 152: Do you watch movies, and how many per month?

I don't watch television, don't have cable and will go to a real theatre about two times a year. When I do watch a film, it's likely to be older. If my husband and kids tell me about a movie that I absolutely must watch, or if we make the decision to take the plunge with a new one, it's going to be happy, family-friendly and guarantee me a good ending.

The reason for my choice is simple: I'm a very visual person. When I see a violent image, it bothers me greatly. Around the time I had my son, in my early twenties, I developed a strong aversion to violence, as well as bad language. It brings me down, I feel dark, and I can't write at all. As time has gone on, I've found that to be a productive writer and produce uplifting work, I must be those things myself. The way I maintain that is to avoid books or visuals that are going to bring me down.

Question 153: Do you give out copies of your books as gifts?

No. I feel its presumptive to assume a person's genre of choice, and egotistical on my part to think they even care about my book. The few times I gave away copies were to relatives (early on). I later learned they never cracked open the first page. That did it.

Question 154: Have you met any other famous authors?

A few, but mostly picture book authors who have been at the same events as myself, on panels or signing books. We usually banter about what books we have read recently, which devolves into a hushed conversation about how few books we are actually reading.

Question 155: How much time do you spend on research before you start writing?

For my non-fiction, it will range from three months to a year, particularly if I'm interviewing dozens of people. It takes a lot of time to meet, schedule and conduct multiple interviews. For the Sue Kim project, it took three years of research and interviewing, following by another year of fact-checking. My women's fiction takes very little research time because the plotline is romantic and the settings are places where I've been. The genre that takes the longest is my YA action-adventure because those plot lines involve historical locations and figures. It takes a minimum of six months research or longer.

Question 156: Do you write all of your books in the same genres you read?

No, not really. Part of this stems from my ever-present concern that I will be copying another author's idea, so I tend to shy away from women's fiction. But I love thrillers, suspense, biographies, fantasy, sci-fi and all sorts of non-fiction. Peter's advice to read all types of things and write in various styles to stay sharp is always on replay, so whenever I feel I'm getting stale I force myself to mix it up.

Much of my non-fiction writing is the result my desire to help others in a way that I would have appreciated when I started out, either in business or as an author. I don't expect this to ever change.

Question 157: Will you stay a writer the rest of your life?

Yes. When I was running around the track in 8th grade, I was making up stories to get through the pain of the half-miler. Later, in college and then in business meetings, my mind continued to wander. It can't be stopped, like the music that flows from a composer or the artist who must draw. It is who I am.

Question 158: How do you handle a bad review?

It depends on the day, my mood and the context of the review. Sometimes the reviews are incredibly valuable. One woman wrote a review where she noted my obsession with watches when referring to a particular character. I could understand why this would become annoying after a while—a few references were okay, but beyond that it grated.

As an author, I've known people who are completely obsessed with watches (my father) or other accessories, like sunglasses (Jennifer Aniston). It is a part of their character. However, I learned from this commentary and paid attention in my next book to add color to help define the character but made sure not to overdo it.

Thank you anonymous reader. You actually improved my writing.

Question 159: What's the most stressful part of writing?

The day before and the day I begin writing a new book. I literally get an upset stomach and have serious diarrhea that continues for about the first ten pages. Then, miraculously, the stress, nerves and stomach pains leave and they never come back. Not until after the book is finished, and I start on the next one. It's never changed, by the way, no matter how many books I write. I tell myself I'm not strange. I know NBA players who get adrenaline shakes before each game and professional singers who live in the bathroom before each performance. I suppose it's no different. The body responds to the mind's adrenaline in a variety of ways.

Question 160: What's the most satisfying part of writing?

The most satisfying part of writing is when a reader, whom I don't know, tells me he/she cried in a certain part, and I'll remember crying when I wrote that part—I feel like that reader is a part of me and I'm a part of the reader. Or a reader will say how and why they identified with a character, and how the person came alive to them, and I will know exactly what they mean, because it's the way I felt when writing that person, or when a reader says they could visualize a foreign city because of the way I wrote about it.

Experiences like that validate my time and effort and in a way, I feel much closer to the reader than I often feel towards relatives. It's so much more meaningful to me than a few dollars I get on a book sale—incomparable really.

Question 161: Should I subscribe to *Publishers Weekly*?

Sure, why not? I don't any longer, and here's why. Early on, I read the pages with a hopeful innocence, envisioning myself one day in the deal section. I used this visual as inspiration, which worked for a few months. As time went on, reading about the successes of other authors started to depress me. I realized it would be years until that would happen to me, if ever. Instead of spending my free time in the bathtub, on the treadmill, couch or wherever, reading about others, I needed to concentrate on improving my craft. That day, I cancelled my subscription and haven't renewed it since.

Question 162: How much time do you spend writing versus marketing and sales?

Until a year ago, it was 90/10, authoring versus spending time on the other aspects of the writing business. With each book that's come out, the time spent on writing has been reduced. It's now 60/40 and depending on the week, lopsided in the other direction. This last week, as the manuscript started to wrap up and the marketing machine increased, it was literally zero writing.

Early on this troubled me, because I felt like I wasn't being dedicated and my craft would suffer. Now I'm more pragmatic. Until

I hire out certain parts of the business, which I elect not to do, then I will be forced to balance out the writing and the business of authoring.

Question 163: Do you hire out your social media activities?

No. I understand the temptation and why authors (and other public figures) do this, but I'm uncomfortable with another person representing me, putting words in my mouth, commenting on subjects or people in a way that is not me. It's one thing to respond to a request to participate in an event, but another matter entirely when the individual on the other end believes it's me they're speaking with. I want to make sure I keep that trust-based relationship, and farming it out is a break.

Question 164: Do you have any author oddities that actually work?

Working is in the eye of the beholder, but readers are purchasing my books, so that indicates to me that at least some of my oddities are beneficial or "working."

- **Prayer**

I pray before I plan and write my books. I get a sense of peace out of the process, and feel like I'm being guided by something bigger than myself. Call it mental or real, the fact is my writing flows better as a result.

➢ **Thinking about my younger self**

When writing fiction, I cast myself into the role(s) of certain characters, and write to my younger self, the person I wanted to be, and wasn't. In my non-fiction, I do the same thing, but the information usually centers on helping others. The primary goal is always this: what did I want to know when I was younger that no one tell me. That drives nearly all of my non-fiction work.

➢ **Music**

When I am writing action-adventure, it's upbeat, trance music, the type with few words but lots of beats. Non-fiction is nearly always classical and women's contemporary fiction is chill out and groove melodic. It's almost always a European station, one that remind me of my travels and instantly transports me.

Question 165: What's the biggest downside of being an author?

Absolute loneliness.

I'm not talking about the vocation, as in "writing is a lonely vocation," because I disagree with that sentiment. So many hours are spent talking with people on the business side (completely discounting the interviews for non-fiction works) that an author has plenty of interaction with others. I'm talking about the loneliness that comes from the social circle that constricts in direct correlation with success.

I touched on this in the first part of the book, which I attribute to the paranoia and jealously of others in response to my success. Whatever the cause, it is the winter freeze that never thaws. It's taken many years to get used to it, and I was helped quite a bit by a bestselling author with three dozen books under her belt. She's in her early sixties at this point, lives in a beautiful, big house with her now-retired husband and dotes on her dogs when she's not writing.

"I take great pleasure in giving complete strangers all my attention," she said. "And they in turn, give me more virtual affection and friendship than anyone I know."

I must say that is true. Thanks to social media, immediate, genuine appreciation is quickly felt and it's uplifting. Are these actual friends? Some have become real-life friends, believe it or not, which is wonderful. Instagram, in particular, has been a great boon to alleviating the loneliness. IG isn't political like Twitter, and not laced with the bitter-weirdness of Facebook. Whatever the case, my personal life is less lonely than it was, and I'm also more at peace with the singular downside of this wonderful vocation.

Question 166: Did you have an event that triggered your change in attitude?

Eventually, I moved from worrying about being judged to growing tired of it and today, I find the best way to end the subject really fast is to either say nothing or come right out and be super blunt, as I did with at a dinner party last month.

I was sitting amongst teachers, nurses (one getting her Ph.D.

while working full-time) and a hedge-fund manager who was also an ultra-marathoner, their spouses and partners. The conversation circled to and fro, touching on each person's vocation over the course of three hours. I am genuinely curious about other people and kept them all talking about themselves, but eventually the question turned to me. I self-identified as an author, and the hedge fund manager said nothing, while his wife (the nurse-Ph.D. candidate), smirked, and said, "Do you like staying home? Are you good at it?"

> You are an author, a public figure. You are going to be judged no matter what you write, so live your life in a way that's pleasing and congruent to your soul.

At that moment something clicked, and I decided to be as straightforward and as proud of my vocation as she was when she said she was working full time as a nurse and getting her Ph.D. (which, by the way, had greatly impressed me).

I said this:

"Well, I have nine books published in sixteen countries and four languages. A couple have been optioned for movies and I just signed an off-Broadway musical agreement. So, I don't mind staying at home doing what I love."

Her look of shock and the slight adjustment in the tenor of the room was worth feeling a little uncomfortable, and I realized something. **No one else hides what they do for a living, nor do they shy away from announcing they won a marathon or an award, so why should I?** As an author, I'm going to be judged for what I write, what I don't write and because I'm a "public figure," I'm open to all sorts of criticism and nasty things that aren't allowed for "private individuals." I might as well be as loud and proud of my profession as everyone else at the dinner party.

Question 167: Do you have any authors that you look to emulate (how they produce their content and control their brand)?

No, not really. I certainly consume a lot of information about what's going on the industry, but I will tell you that watching other authors is like reading *Publishers Weekly*. It becomes distracting as I focus on what they are doing and pay less attention to what I should be doing, like writing, building my library and creating sales programs that will sell books.

That said, I have always admired John Grisham for his ability to ignore the naysayers, who were many and vigorous, about his writing for years. Early on, he endured what I figured was about nine years of absolute thrashing by the media. I recall reading *People Magazine* in particular (as a high school student) who wrote about his bad writing, simple plots, thin sentences, and just about every other negative thing they could find. I also recall when this changed, seemingly overnight. From the east coast literary critics to the mainstream media, his work was derided until his tremendous book sales and then movies essentially shut them up. When I read a bad review of one of my books, or am on the receiving end of judgement or criticism about my writing career, I think about Grisham, who, as far as I could tell, just kept his head down, ignored everyone and kept writing. That worked for him, me for me or anyone else.

Admire the habits and accomplishments of other authors, but not to the extent it depresses or distracts you from accomplishing your own goals.

Question 168: What skills do you recommend newbie authors develop ASAP?

Patience and persistence, and don't confuse those two with laziness, complacency or bull-headedness.

When I say patience, I am referring to the state of mind that wills you to slow down on editing, to not rush through the back-jacket cover text, to take your time when you are fact checking. Patience also means that give your agent or publisher the time to market your book (you don't hound them unnecessarily), because certain elements of editing Simply, Take, Time. You can't speed them up, nor should you try.

Persistence doesn't mean being aggressive and annoying, or shutting out your family, friends or putting off important obligations as you write the great American novel. It means that on a consistent and constant basis, you make choices that forward your dream. Every spare five minutes you have, be it waiting in the car or at the dental office, between making dinner or on the train ride home, you are taking advantage of the time and applying it towards your dream. No, you don't have to have your computer or a notepad with you every second. Half of my "writing," is done mentally, when I'm thinking through scenes and the exact wording of a sentence.

Question 169: Would you personally collaborate with any authors in the future?

Unlikely, and I'll explain, because I didn't used to think this way. It evolved after several experiences that convinced me I'm a good mentor and advisor but wouldn't be a good collaborator.

If you recall Chapter Nine, I related that collaboration is one of the ways to earn income. To that point, I had been approached two times to collaborate on a book. The first time was by a very nice, very reclusive man, who essentially wanted both of our names on a series of books for a topic of interest to him. The subject was of some interest to me, and it was non-fiction and the books would be short, 200-page how-to guides. He had the contacts: dozens of well-places executives who had previously not spoken to the press on the topic(s) at hand, and it would have dramatically expanded my network.

My biggest concern, and the reason I ultimately declined the project, was because it wasn't core to my area of interest. When I write non-fiction, I do so because I truly love the subject matter. It's taking away from writing fiction, which I love more.

Another time, I was approached to collaborate on a work of fiction, with a well-known author who had a vision that I would ultimately take over her line of fiction books. We'd both have our name on the top, but after a while, she'd phase out of the writing process. She'd sit back and collect money (the scale would slide over time) and I'd get the immediate value and impact of her name and brand, which was, and still is, far greater than my own.

I wasn't interested in this because I was unwilling to give up my own ideas for someone else's. No amount of money or fame was worth keeping all those ideas inside my head.

Question 170: How do you help other authors who you like, but don't want to collaborate with?

Earlier in the book, I wrote about reading the works of aspiring authors, which I still do on occasion. The decision I make to spend the time on reading or not reading is a gradual and very personal one, typically based on the rapport I have with that person. Like anyone else, I'm drawn in by engaging personalities or an earnest nature where I can tell the individual is honest and sincere. That's more compelling than anything else (e.g. offers of money), which do nothing for me.

When a person connects with me, I've done quite a few things for them, outside of reading a first draft. I've introduced a half-dozen to potential agents, editors, publishing houses, and even individuals for networking needs. Sometimes, the desires are totally outside the world of publishing, and I have no hesitation to opening the right doors to someone who I believe can make a difference.

And that's really what it boils down to. At my core, I believe that we can all make a difference, that we are placed here on this earth to accomplish wonderful things. Not everyone thinks this way, and approaches life with vigor and a desire to have an impact. So, when I come across a person who shares this sentiment, I believe it's my moral duty to help that person get as far along as fast as possible.

Question 171: Any other genres you would seriously consider exploring and why?

Spoiler alert! My first serious novels were in the suspense category, back when I thought I wanted to be the next Robert Ludlum. Yet my journey began with young adult action/adventure/suspense, then moved to women's fiction. The common denominator is fast-paced and a trend towards suspense-oriented themes.

I can see a day where I might continue this evolution to suspense books, but it's not clear if I'd add this as a new genre or if I'd incorporate those themes into my women's contemporary fiction. At this point, I genres I won't ever explore, such as fantasy, sci-fi, true crimes etc. While I like elements of each, I don't think I'm creative enough for fantasy, smart enough for sci-fi, or mentally strong enough for true crime! That said, I greatly admire many authors in each of those genres.

Question 172: Do you write on holiday?

Writing, no, but idea building, yes. Specifically, I'll write on my laptop during the flight over and back, but from the moment I land to liftoff, I'm *idea building*. Idea building is the concept of being open to a new idea, or taking the kernel of one concept and developing every aspect of the storyline. That, to me, is fun, exciting and wonderful, everything a vacation should be. I take my notebook everywhere, since I've lost data stored on my phone one too many times.

Question 173: If your book is getting made into a film, do you have any say? Why or why not?

Very few authors have a vote in the details of how a film is made. Having signed two film option agreements and worked with producing companies in the industry for nearly a decade, I know this is common. The best that can be hoped for, most of the time, is to have "input."

> You write the book, the filmmaker creates the movie. You can sit back and support the process or you can try to interject your opinions in a field you know nothing about. There is no in between.

The reason, I was told time and again, can be traced back to an incident in the eighties, when one of the bestselling authors of that era (and still today) signed an option for his film. He demanded, and got, the final green light approval for most aspects of the film. As legend goes, he disagreed on every actor suggested by the director and producer. That was eventually overcome, but when he disagreed on set changes (due to budget considerations), objected to the way the dialogue was modified to fit the scene, thereby not being true to the book and so on. Some were reasonable objections, others were absurd.

It got so bad that project went through two directors. As the author refused to agree to suggested changes, the studio refused to capitulate to his demands, and after spending over fifty million dollars—a huge sum at the time—production was shut down. The author has never, not once, had one of his books brought to the big screen, and based upon all the filmmakers I've spoken to in the industry, he never will.

Since that time, only a handful of author's have received final say status. J.K. Rowling is the singular example everyone cites. Another is Stephenie Meyer, who received an increased level of control in the Twilight series. Both Stephen King and John Grisham demanded, and received, certain sign-off stipulations. Without naming specific films, it was an open secret that both were unhappy about their adaptations. As each demanded final say, the studios balked, and you can see how the demand to bring their books to the big screen has largely dropped off.

An author is an expert in the written word. The author must make a choice: to either trust and support the filmmaker's approach or not have a film made at all.

It comes down to this. Filmmakers are supposed to be experts in bringing a story to life visually. Few studios want to risk millions of dollars in a production that can be handcuffed by an irrational author—and trust me, most filmmakers I have worked with think us authors are just that, irrational.

Question 174: Have you ever had an editor, publisher or director force you to include changes or modify your stories in ways that you have objected to?

Yes, I've had every single person at every level and in every role in publishing ask to change parts of the books I've written. It starts at the agent level (increase the pace here, drop this character out of the story line), then at the acquisitions editor (cut this entire storyline out) and the publisher (change the voice of the entire book). Then at the movie level (change the voice from 3rd to first person, age up the characters from 14 to 18, extend the plot line from three books to five).

In terms of my objecting to suggestions, I'm an open-minded person and have always been interested in hearing the opinion of 'an expert' until that person shows that their aren't relying upon data or statistics or prior experience, but giving me personal opinions. Early on, with the non-fiction, I pretty much had to do whatever McGraw-Hill wanted. They had the data, statistics, facts and figures, that showed their proven format would sell more books. Also, it was my first book deal and I had no basis for comparison. Did I hate it? Parts of it, yes. I wanted to write first person, they required third. I had tons of wonderful stories of failure, my own and executives who had gone on the record with me to share their own growth experiences, all of which got cut. I learned from writing that book, and made different choices for future non-fiction works.

Fiction, once again, is entirely different. Before a deal is even signed, the acquisition editor is straight forward about what he/she wants added or cut. The suggested changes have included: adding in more swearing, more sex, alternative lifestyles, more drama, angst, more pages, or deleting thirty thousand words. You name it, I've gotten it. In fact, some requests are super specific. One editor told me if I wanted to write chick lit, I needed to have sex in the first three pages, and about every twenty pages thereafter. Note that I've never written a chick-lit book.

The good news is that this comes up before you sign the publishing contract, and you are either on board with making the required changes or not.

Movies are more collaborative in nature, I'd say. While the studio is developing a five movie franchise based on what I've already written, discussions are going on about what I have yet to write. The producer of *Chambers* wanted to change the setting for Book one due to a concern that the location wouldn't be as globally appealing to the target audience. I'd already researched the historical facts and designed the entire five-story plot line around certain elements of Book two. This included foreshadowing in Book one. I dug in my heels and kept the location.

However, for Book three, the situation was different. The crew was concerned about other things, such as safety of the cast and crew, budget. I could see the merit of changing the location, and since it was early enough in the writing process, I agreed to recast the setting.

It took me nearly six months to completely recraft the plot, sub-plots and characters to make it work with a new location, not to mention all the additional research I had to do associated with the historical figures.

Am I happy with it? Yes, and I agree with the producer that the change made for a better product. Did it completely and utterly throw me off for a solid year? Yep. It sure did, and on top of all of that, I've had a lot of reader complaints questioning my ability to finish the series. Well, these things take time, and I wasn't comfortable sharing the behind-the-scenes drama with the world. Now you know.

Question 175: Have you ever had any problems with crazy readers or people you've written about?

Unfortunately, yes, and it's still going on to this day. It all started with the release of *Chambers*, which has proven to be just as interesting to

35 yr-old men as it is for the youth audience it was written for. In fact, over the last number of years, I have gotten more comments, emails and feedback of all sorts from this older category regarding *Chambers*. It has been completely surprising to me, but not as much as the fact that I've become the recipient of full-on harassment and stalking.

At first, Roger and I thought local kids were jumping our meager little fence and coming on the property (on five acres in a neighborhood about 10 minutes outside the closest city). Then we noticed lights were being turned off in our absence. One evening, I was sleeping downstairs (it was super hot in our bedroom) and I looked up to see a person standing at the foot of my bed. In my half awake state I said, "Rog, what are you doing up?" and I went back to sleep. Sometime later, I woke again and saw the same silhouette and this time was irritated. "Rog, what are you doing?" I started to sit up. The figure ran towards the door, and as I started hyperventilating, the person ran out of the house.

A few things happened after that. We put up six foot high, solid fencing around the property, a huge privacy gate and activated the alarm system at night, which we'd never done before. We got our first dog ever, a pit bull, who later on saved us from an attack (I'll save that for another book), but you know what? The harassment continued.

We moved states, not necessarily to escape the craziness, but we figured that would be a side benefit. Not so. Somehow, this person tracked down my privately-listed address and phone number, and I have received packages, letters and calls. So has my agent, friends and relatives in other states.

Before this experience, I naively thought that an author had to be of the Stephenie Meyer fame level to attract this type of crazy. Further, I had little or no sympathy for reports of individuals having to contend with a harasser or stalker, falling back on the notion that 'people in the public eye know very well what they are getting into.'

Well, I write in one of my books, "We mock that which we don't understand, and then we get to experience it ourselves."

The lesson I've learned the hard way is that an author should expect the unexpected.

Question 176: How do you deal with a person who strongly objects with something you've written in fiction or non-fiction?

You can either ignore the criticism or respond. On Goodreads and other sites, they advise authors to ignore bad reviews and criticism, because the dialogue devolves into a shouting match. I agree with the advice in this context. Criticism or a bad review is the right of the reader and is free speech. It's when the criticism bleeds over into full-on personal insults or unjustified slander that action must be taken.

In the authorized biography of Sue Kim, a number of people had addictions or characteristics that were described in an unpleasing light. As a result, two individuals have continued to harass me about changing the content. Since I was given eye-witness accounts from multiple sources that contradicted the requested changes from said individuals, I ignored the emails, letters and phone calls that first went to myself, then my agent, then publisher and so on. In one case, a man claimed credit as the PR agent for getting the Kim Sisters on the Ed Sullivan show. But when I interviewed the talent manager, band manager and others, all identified another source entirely who had made that happen. In that case as well, I ignored the individual.

The downside of this strategy meant that the requests turned threatening.

Demand for a change in the manuscript morphed into threats of a lawsuit, then this person contacting Amazon (all the way up to Jeff Bezos if you can believe, which I didn't at first, until I saw the emails with Amazon's attorney), to get my book pulled from the shelf (yes! This really happens). After a review of the situation, Amazon declined to do anything (which means I won with facts) and then the switch flipped. This led into personal insults about me, my writing, etc. Ultimately, after three years, I finally took a stand and responded, in writing, to the issues presented. I explained how I used the US Journalism Code of Ethics, the process I followed, the sourcing used, as well as the interviewees reading and approval of all quotes prior to printing. I also identified that my role, as the author, was not to insert my opinions or emotions. What was written (in the narrative) was limited to the scenes, setting the tone, flow etc. All the quotes were included word for word, not loose interpretations of sentiments.

Has this helped at all, you might ask? A little. I receive fewer emails and letters, but it comes up now and then on social media and

Amazon reviews, where you can clearly see the person is disgruntled and angry at me, the author. And yes, I get sick to my stomach when I'm attacked because it's unjustified. It takes a few days, but I eventually get centered again. But I will say that during those days where I'm unbalanced, I can't write at all. I'm worthless and know it. So, I try to eat right (and not inhale every bit of chocolate in sight), and be positive and productive until I'm in my happy zone again. PS. I don't always succeed.

Question 177: How do you keep your feet on the ground if you find success?

Trick question? No matter how I answer this, it's guaranteed to cause ire, so I'm going to be my usual, honest self.

We went backwards in the face of success. Six years ago, when my husband sold his latest software company and my writing started to take off, we didn't want to fall into the trap of more consumption, bigger house, more cars, etc. We made the decision to move from the big city to the small one. In the process, we cut our living space in half (e.g. the home is much smaller). He drives a 12-year-old truck and I drive a 5-year-old SUV. We purchase our animals from shelters, we raise our own chickens and eat from our garden.

It's hard to preach sustainable living when you're not doing it, so we adjusted our life accordingly. Was it rough? Very much so. The vision is a lot harder than reality. I can't even get a pair of stockings without crossing the state line into Washington. I kid you not. But our neighbors are legitimate, humble and would give you the shirt of your back. I'll forgo nylons any day of the week for that kind of quality of life for me and my family.

Question 178: How do you keep the quality of your future writing at a high level high if you find success, so that your brand is not ruined?

This question came from a man overseas who was basically asking whether a successful author gets lazy over time and "phones it in," thereby angering the readers and hurting the brand.

This gets to a pet peeve of mine—the author who creates the framework for the book then hires a ghostwriter to write the book. Did you know that a number of bestselling authors do this around book 9 or 10? The brand is built, the readership strong, and the publisher wants the author to write more books. Many times, the publisher is complicit in working with the author to find a ghost writer who matches the author's writing style.

How do I know this? I have four friends who are NYT bestselling authors, who have told me directly this is what they now do. They simply want more free time to enjoy the money and time they have rightly earned. Once again, I go back to James Patterson. At least the man is giving credit to other writers and acknowledges his strategy. I'd rather have that than the dishonesty of thinking you are purchasing an author's book only to learn its been written by someone else.

Question 179: If it is so hard to making a living from writing, why do it in the first place?

It's like the actor who works retail to pay the bills, or the musician who DJs at a radio station during the day. We all have our passions in life that we are going to pursue no matter what. It provides a joy and satisfaction that can't be found anywhere else. Period.

Question 180: Do you ever have moods where you can't write? What do you do about it?

Absolutely. Family or personal issues can leave me emotionally off-balance. When I'm in a funky bad mood, sad or depressed, my work reflects it. I've learned it's easier to not write at all then write crap and have to rewrite or throw it out and start over.

What I do about it depends on the situation. If the issue is simple, I throw myself into exercising for a few hours, go to bed exhausted and wake up the next morning knowing the day will be better. Other times, I actually have to fast and pray a lot (that means I pray, don't eat for a day or so, thereby mentally and spiritually detoxing), and then pick up when I feel centered. Trying to hurry up the process never works. One can't force the mind, body or heart to heal in order to meet a writing deadline.

Question 181: How do you keep it fresh?

By following Peter's advice to mix up my writing. Every third fiction book, I stop and write a non-fiction book (or two). By then, I'm interested in writing fiction again.

Writing articles for local papers, writing a blog, traveling and the like are all factors into keeping it fresh. This last summer, I essentially took off two months because a close family member was diagnosed with inoperable brain cancer. When I wasn't on the emotional roller coaster, I was doing laundry (see how sexy my life is)? Survival mode wasn't conducive to writing anything so I didn't even try. By the time fall came around, the roller coaster had more or less hit the straightaway, the kids were back in school and I felt ready to begin again.

Question 182: How much downtime do you have between writing books?

Assuming no major life issues, I will allow myself a break of between two days up to two weeks to regroup and get geared up for a new project. No more. Experience has taught me that going longer for two weeks makes me lazy. I get out of the habit of writing, my desire to sit in the chair for hours at a time goes away.

Question 183: What do you do during the downtime?

My activities are those where I don't have the opportunity to think about writing. Playing the piano and riding a motorcycle are extremely concentrated activities. A power yoga class is so hard I can't consider anything but breathing so I don't pass out. Those are the things I veer towards.

Question 184: What's your best advice to all writers?

1. Don't listen to the naysayers.
2. Don't give up.
3. Don't alter who you are and what you want to write to satisfy some editor's short-term objectives.
4. Don't sacrifice your long-term dreams for short-term pleasure.
5. Don't sign long-term contracts for multiple books when you are starting out. Limit your contract and book count so you can get more money later, when you hit the big time.

Question 185: What's your biggest regret?

1. That I didn't act on the first inspiration to write when I was in high school, and ignored the second round of inspiration while I was in college. As a result, I essentially lost at least 15 years of writing.
2. That I didn't listen to Peter Rubie earlier. That cost me another 5 years.

My fear, insecurity and stubbornness eliminated twenty years of writing potential. It's the reason why I tell you over and over to **start writing, do it now, and don't stop**. Don't look back and wish for those twenty years like I do. Time is the one thing you can't replace.

KEY REFERENCES

1. *The Elements of Narrative Nonfiction*, Rubie, Peter
2. *100 Ways to Improve your Writing,* Provost, Gary
3. *How to Write a Movie in 21 Days*, King, Vickie
4. *The Writer's Digest: Character Naming Sourcebook*: Kenyno, Sherrilyn, Writer's Digest Books
5. *The Observation Deck*, Epel, Naomi
6. *How to Publish, Promote and Sell Your Own Book*, Holt, Robert Lawrence
7. *The Elements of Storytelling*, Rubie, Peter
8. *The art of Fiction*, Gardner, John
9. *The Elements of Style,* by Strunk and White. (Note: it was originally a self-published book!)

INDEX

ABOUT THE AUTHOR

Before she began writing novels, Sarah Gerdes established herself as a recognized expert in the areas of business management and consulting. Her thirteen books have been published in sixteen countries and translated into four languages. Two have been optioned for film and another for a musical.

ACKNOWLEDGEMENTS

The greats who have been influential in my life over the last two decades. Mark C. who read my first book and didn't kill the dream. Peter Rubie, with his great advice, patience and ability to fire me and take me back. My two primary editors, Pam Liflander and Jennifer Fischer, who took the time to teach me while editing my work. All these people have kicked me in the butt when I needed it, and I'm forever grateful. Erika Spry must be called out, because it was she who launched this book by giving me a few too many questions to answer. Finally, Andy Thomas and Rachel Parker deserve a special mention, because when I get down, depressed or despondent, I think of these two aspiring authors. Their fortitude to keep going despite their odds is what actually inspires me. Thank you both. You are amazing.

OTHER BOOKS

Fiction- Women's Contemporary
A Convenient Date
Made for Me (Book 1 in the Danielle Grant series)
Destined for You (Book 2 in the Danielle Grant series)
In a Moment

Fiction- Action Adventure
Chambers (Book 1 in the Chambers Series)
Chamber: The Spirit Warrior (Book 2 in the Chambers Series)

Non-Fiction
The Overlooked Expert: Turning your skills into a profitable business (10th Anniversary Edition)
Sue Kim: The Authorized Biography. The greatest American story never told
Navigating the Partnership Maze: Creating alliances that work

01162018a

Made in the USA
Columbia, SC
10 April 2021

35899682R00176